JEWELRY
& Accessories

JEWELRY
& Accessories

Beautiful designs to make and wear

JULIET BAWDEN

Photography by James Duncan

NORTH LIGHT BOOKS
Cincinnati, Ohio

Dedication
For Diana and Chris Wilkinson

First published in North America in 1994
by North Light Books, an imprint of F&W Publications,
1507 Dana Avenue, Cincinnati, Ohio 45207.
1-800-289-0963.

Reprinted 1996

First Published in 1994
by Letts of London
an imprint of New Holland (Publishers) Ltd
London · Cape Town · Sydney

ISBN 0 89134 654 6

New Holland (Publishers) Ltd
Chapel House, 24 Nutford Place,
London W1H 6DQ

Designed and edited by
Anness Publishing Limited

Printed and bound in Hong Kong by
South China Printing Co Ltd

Contents

Introduction

While researching this book, I came across some very old, quaint manuals which stated in no uncertain terms that jewellery was formed from precious metals and gemstones and that anything other than this was not entitled to call itself jewellery. Happily, we now live in more enlightened times when the boundaries between art, design and craftsmanship have become blurred. To reflect these new ideas, this book takes a broader approach to the subject, including metalwork and other traditional skills together with many contemporary techniques not usually associated with jewellery-making.

The strong international interest in all crafts has influenced the way many people perceive jewellery and all forms of decorative adornment. Jewellery is one of the most popular collectables, encompassing a huge variety of styles from traditional to modern, ethnic to classic, and ranging from the reasonably priced impulse buy to the once-in-a-lifetime investment. Jewellery-making is an ideal craft to take up as it requires very little space and, depending on which project you choose to make, the tools and equipment need not cost a great deal. You may even find you have discovered a money-making hobby.

This book begins with an historical overview, tracing the origins of jewellery from the ancient civilizations of Egypt and Mesopotamia to today's wide-ranging fashions. It discusses the various styles of jewellery, and how to choose shapes and colours to suit your look and personality. The gallery section features a truly inspirational collection of contemporary jewellery, some of which is made using the techniques described in the book. The project section, Creating Jewellery and Accessories, includes a wide range of stylish, individual and innovative designs for earrings, necklaces, rings, bracelets and brooches. The pieces have all been designed by artists who work professionally in their given fields and each project has been carefully planned with step-by-step photographs showing every stage.

There are also many quick and easy-to-follow ideas for embellishing clothing and creating simple items of jewellery and accessories from everyday materials, and there is a comprehensive section detailing the materials, equipment and techniques.

With something for everyone, from the novice to the experienced craftsperson looking for new ideas and inspiration, this books contains everything you need to set you on the way to designing and making original and stylish jewellery for yourself and, if you can bear to give it away, for your family and friends.

Historical overview

Jewellery is the answer to our profound need for self-adornment and is consequently one of the oldest forms of decorative art. There is evidence of the existence of beads in the early civilizations of Egypt and Mesopotamia (Iraq) 7,000 years ago, although the earliest known jewellery is thought to date from Neanderthal times and is believed to be 40,000 years old. This jewellery – a hoard of beads made from animal bones and teeth – was discovered in La Quina in France.

Jewellery has also been worn to show the status and wealth of the wearer. For instance, in medieval Europe, laws and decrees proclaimed that only certain classes of society could wear particular categories of jewellery. In many cultures, jewellery is worn for amuletic or protective purposes. For example, in ancient China, jade was believed to have spiritual qualities.

Egyptian jewellery

As the Egyptians were buried in their everyday jewellery, it has been difficult for historians to distinguish between funerary, amuletic and secular jewellery. The materials used, as well as the forms carved into them, had great significance. For example, red carnelian was the colour of life blood, green feldspar or turquoise meant new life, and blue lapis lazuli was the colour of the heavens. Falcon or bull amulets gave the owners the power of assimilation, while other amulets, such as the scorpion, represented something to be avoided. Many amulets had holes carved into them so they could be worn as beads.

The high point of Egyptian jewellery was during the Middle Kingdom (about 2040–1730 BC). Goldwork was carried out using techniques including granulation, repoussé and chasing, while cloisonné work was developed to sophisticated levels. Lapis lazuli, carnelian, amethyst, green feldspar and turquoise were favourite stones, and strings of metal-capped beads, often graded in size, also appeared.

North-west European jewellery

The culmination in early Bronze Age metalworking from the period 1400–600 BC is believed to be the great gold cape, a mastery of the techniques of beating out and embossing on a large scale, found at Torc in North Wales. In contrast to mainland Europe, very little jewellery has been found in burial grounds in Britain and Ireland from this period, leading historians to believe that much of what we consider jewellery today was in fact made for a special purpose rather than for purely decorative embellishment.

Celtic bronze and enamel terret from the first century AD. Bronze was the most popular material for jewellery-making during this period and was often enriched with other materials such as coral or enamel. (*Above: Christie's, London*)

Collection of medieval rings, all made from gold. Note the different settings – some very crude in construction, others much finer. Two of the rings bear the wearers' insignias. (*Right: Christie's, London*)

Collection of jewellery from the eighth century BC to third century AD, mostly Egyptian, some Roman, including a scarab and an amulet. As the examples here show, most jewellery of this period was made in gold. (*Above: Christie's, London*)

*R*are medieval
cameo, a
precious or semi-
precious stone on
which a design is
carved in relief. The
design is usually a bust;
figures such as these
are less common.
c. thirteenth or four-
teenth century.
(*Above: Christie's,
London*)

Phoenician jewellery

During the period 850–325 BC, the Phoeni-cians were both traders and colonists. They carried the jewellery of Western Asia throughout the Mediterranean region, and it is sometimes hard to distinguish between their own work and that of the native Europeans who learned jewellery-making skills from them and imitated their styles. A distinctive characteristic of Phoenician jewellery is the use of decorative motifs derived from Egypt.

Greek jewellery

The great Mycenaean civilization came to an end in 1100 BC and was followed by several centuries of widespread poverty when jewellery was very rare. By 850 BC, contacts with Western Asia had resumed, resulting in greater prosperity and a revival in Greek jewellery which was to last until 600 BC. From 850–700 BC there were important centres for goldwork in Knossos, Corinth and Athens.

Etruscan jewellery

Early Etruscan jewellery, dating from around 500 BC, is characterized by its abundance, its technical perfection and its variety. The Etruscans loved colour, and their necklaces were a combination of deli-cately granulated gold beads, and glass and faience beads of Phoenician origin.

Celtic jewellery

The principal piece of Celt jewellery was the torc or neck ring. It was mentioned by classical writers as being worn by warriors in battle. However, these rings have only been found around the necks of women and girls in Celtic tombs. They were prob-ably used as a form of currency rather than for personal adornment.

Medieval times to the nineteenth century

Medieval jewellery is characterized by its highly stylized animal forms and geometric designs. The latter half of the fourteenth century was notable for lavish expenditure on jewellery with a strong French influence and dominant religious motifs. During Renaissance times, religious imagery was replaced largely by mythological and alle-gorical figures.

Diamond jewellery as we know it today first developed in the seventeenth century when rose-cutting was invented in Holland in 1640. Brilliant cutting by Venetians at the close of that century meant that for the first time the gem became more important than the mount.

The eighteenth century saw many changes, for the English style was over-whelmed by a lighter and more fanciful rococo style, which in turn was followed by a classical revival. The Victorian period followed, with its over-ornate and often sentimental designs.

*V*ictorian necklace of diamonds and rubies. Note the leaf shapes which turn the hanging rubies set in two circles of diamonds into flowers.
(*Right*: *Christie's, London*)

*L*alique necklace made from flower-shaped dark blue glass beads. In the centre, a Lalique dark green glass pendant; turn of the century.
(*Right*: *Christie's, London*)

*A*rt Nouveau buckles and brooches made from silver inlaid with blue and green enamel and mother of pearl. Note the flowing forms and the natural imagery.
(*Right*: *author's collection*)

The twentieth century

Fashions in jewellery have mirrored those of the major art movements during the twentieth century. Art Nouveau, with its flowing natural forms, was the predominant style at the turn of the century. Buckles, brooches, necklaces and buttons were usually fashioned from silver rather than gold and often finished with green and turquoise enamel. The movement came to an abrupt halt at the outbreak of the First World War.

The French fashion designer Coco Chanel was responsible for the fashion in costume jewellery in the 1920s and 1930s. At the same time, Elsa Schiaparelli, a witty French designer, produced innovative designs for clothes, jewellery and accessories. With the 1930s came Art Deco and strong geometric shapes. New materials such as plastic and bakelite spawned new designs. The 1950s were dominated by Christian Dior and the style was for traditional and pretty pieces.

The new-found freedom of the 1960s influenced jewellery design with op art, plastic, flower power and cow bells. The 1970s were full of nostalgia, especially for paste jewellery, and the famous jewellery emporium of Butler and Wilson opened in London. The 1980s and 1990s have seen a variety of styles, including sophisticated and bizarre jewellery, and jewellery made using non-traditional materials. This is mainly due to the strong artist/designer and craft movement which has developed over the same period.

Folk traditions

The Chinese beads shown here were strung sometime between 1850–1870. The green ones are jade and the cream ones ivory. The earrings are also made from jade. (*Right*: loaned by *Ann Scampton*)

Folk traditions in jewellery are bound up with history, but fashions in jewels as well as other areas of design are often inspired by ethnic as well as historical influences and thereby merit a mention of their own.

Along the 3,000-mile stretch of land between Zaire and the West African coast lies an equatorial rain belt. It is from this region that some of the most valuable and finely-wrought jewellery comes, including carved ivory, cast bronze, gold and glass beads. The people of the rainforest derived their wealth from trade. At the beginning of the fifteenth century, gold and unworked ivory was taken via the Saharan trade routes to the North African coast and exchanged with Portuguese sea traders for glass beads, copper, brass and coral.

In many African cultures, even today, beads are worn to signify the age or status of the wearer. In her book *Africa Adorned*, Angela Fisher tells how most nomadic tribes of East Africa are ordered into an age-set system, their body adornment providing an outward sign of their age and status. Women of the Masai tribe wear flat collars made of beads spaced with strips of cow hide, but only married women are permitted to wear the long blue beads, known as *nborro*, or the beaded snuff containers hung around their necks.

Married Toposa women are distinguished by their hairstyles of tiny pigtails finished with red seed beads. Beaded corsets provide everyday wear for some Dinka men, and the colour of the beads shows their age-set – red and black for 15–25-year-olds, pink and purple for the 25–30 age group, and yellow for those over 30. Attractive beaded bodices are worn by Dinka women who are eligible for marriage, with the patterns of the beads indicating the family's wealth.

Man's recognition of the intrinsic quality of certain materials such as precious metals and gems has led to their constant use in cultures separated by both time and distance. For example, gold, as one of the most precious metals, has been in continual use in totally unconnected cultures. Interestingly, however, the people of the Sahara prefer silver to gold – the metal of the devil – which is feared and believed to bring bad luck.

On the Indian sub-continent, jewellery is also bound up with status, wealth and symbolism. Indian women often wear anklets, wristlets, armlets and bracelets, and may wear nose-rings with a long ornate chain attached. I was once told by an Indian that any jewellery which is not at least 18 carats is considered to be costume jewellery. The importance of this is that a woman has her wealth in her jewellery, a man has his in land.

The fine beads known as rocailles were and still are used by Native Americans in bead-weaving and by South Africans in their beadwork to create a wide range of intricate and colourful effects.

Many of the styles of beads and jewellery from other cultures have been translated into modern designs. Look at old jewellery in museums of ethnography – you may be surprised at just how modern some of it appears to be.

*I*n Africa, amber is prized for its colour, size and magical healing properties. The multi-coloured glass beads are known as trade beads. The metal beads are Berber in origin. (*Left*: *Janet Coles Beads and loaned by Deirdre Hawken*)

*A*ll these pieces of jewellery are made from Indian silver. They consist of a heavy collar, two arm decorations and two hair decorations, all tied together in the traditional way with string. (*Left*: *loaned by Ali Wiser*)

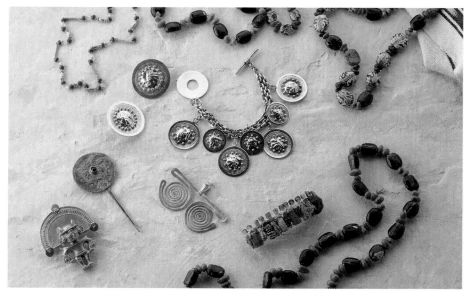

*T*his collection of beads and jewellery from all over the South American continent is typified by the use of indigenous materials and traditional designs. The beads at top right are painted coffee beans. The silver bracelet and earrings are made from coins. The hair clip is made from tiny fabric dolls. (*Left*: *Janet Coles Beads and Inca*)

Designing jewellery

*T*his collection of shoes expresses the sea in both colour, form and imagery and shows how themes can be carried through from jewellery to other accessories. Shells, starfish and sea horses are a recurrent theme, as are the colours of the sea – blue, green and coral.
(*Above: Claire Dennis*)

It is important that each piece of jewellery is designed and made to fit its purpose. Some pieces, such as brooches, clasps, buckles, cuff links and hat pins, are utilitarian as they serve the purpose of fastening clothing. Rings, pendants, necklaces, bracelets and earrings are used solely for personal adornment. This means that the design is of prime importance rather than the materials used for making them.

Design considerations

A ring is usually circular because it fits over the finger. For this reason it should be smooth inside and, as it will come into contact with other fingers, it is best if it is more or less smooth on the outside as well. If any stone or ornament rises too abruptly or too high above the shank it will interfere with the freedom of the hand. If the ring is too wide, it will be difficult to close the fingers and the ring will become uncomfortable.

The brooch, which was originally designed for holding pieces of clothing together, is now more likely to be used to decorate a jacket lapel or a jersey. It is important that the brooch does not have sharp edges which could snag, and that it has a pin which is both large enough and strong enough to hold the brooch in position. The brooch should not be too heavy or it will not lie against the body, but will droop and point downwards.

The hat pin, if it is to serve its purpose, must be fairly weighty. As it has to bear pressure, it must be of a sufficient thickness to withstand bending.

As cuff buttons or links are designed to do up shirts without buttons on the cuffs, they should be flat and unobtrusive in design so as not to interfere with the wearer's movements. A simple outline shape which offers little resistance when fitting the link in place is best.

Buckles are probably the pieces of jewellery which have more strains inflicted upon them than any other type – the strain of an expanding waistline! If the buckle has a prong, this must move freely and be strong enough to serve its purpose without falling off.

Design themes

With such a wide range of materials and techniques at our disposal, it is often difficult for the beginner to know where to start when it comes to jewellery design. Shape, form, colour and surface texture all come into play.

Natural forms are often the inspiration for an item of jewellery and were the prevailing source of imagery in Art Nouveau. Some natural forms lend themselves to

*T*his collection of jewellery shows very clearly how recurrent themes appear in any sphere of design. In this case, five jewellers working in completely different mediums have chosen sea life as a theme and expressed it in very different ways.
(*Right*)

Contemporary designers

design interpretations more than others, especially those which repeat themselves with increasing and decreasing size such as leaf and flower forms.

Sea shells are a popular motif, and the spiral characteristic of many shells has been a feature of decorative design from time immemorial, using materials as diverse as metal, wood, clay and even paper. The rhythm produced by the spiralling lines has supplied the jewellery designer with many ideas. The sea horse, which almost has the appearance of a mythical beast, has often been used as an inspiration for jewellery and accessories.

Butterflies are another favourite motif with their feeling of balance, harmony of line and proportion, and exquisite colours. These may be translated into many kinds of jewellery from earrings and brooches to hat pins and pendants.

Natural objects do not have to be merely inspirational, they may also form part of the design itself. A pebble, shell or piece of driftwood can easily become part of a stylish piece of jewellery.

Jewellery designers have often trained in other disciplines, thereby infusing traditional jewellery design with their varied craft skills. This means that the design may be technique- or material-, rather than design-led. For example, Lizzie Reakes is a designer of floor coverings, using rag rug techniques, which in turn has led to the design of hand-hooked jewellery. The paper and copper jewellery made by Deirdre Hawken is the work of a theatre designer turned jewellery-maker. Anne-Marie Cadman makes felt hats, papier mâché bowls and printed scarves, as well as papier mâché jewellery. The design team of Lushlobes both trained as theatre designers. Their work, made mainly from polymer clay, is theatrical yet very accessible. Gill Clement, who works with embossed paper, also makes pewter jewellery for the clothes designer Jean Muir.

This brings us neatly to accessories, as Jean Muir is known for her sponsorship of talented artists and craftspeople. One of the reasons that there is a strong revival of interest in both jewellery and accessories is that the boundaries between them have become blurred. By changing the bows on your shoes or by throwing a scarf around your neck, the whole look of an ensemble can be changed at minimal cost. Just think how much more expensive a new outfit would be! Jewellery and accessories are infinitely more versatile than in the past, and there are now many new and exciting materials with which to experiment.

Wearing jewellery

These hat pins are used to create a strong fashion statement by grouping them together rather than just having one to anchor the hat in position. The matching brooch emphasizes 'the look'. (*Right*: *Judy Clayton*)

The expensive items of jewellery that you own are likely to be gold chains, bracelets, earrings or rings with precious stones. These are often gifts with strong sentimental attachments, and transcend the vagaries of fashion to become part of your personality. A piece you love can become your signature piece of jewellery to be worn constantly, even if you change all your other accessories at the drop of a hat. It might be a gold link bracelet which was part of your grandfather's watch chain, your grandmother's engagement ring or a pair of diamond stud earrings you received as an eighteenth birthday present.

In recent years there has been a spate of colour analysis – a system which divides people into groups of Spring, Summer, Autumn or Winter. It is an easy way of defining what colours suit you. To quote Carole Jackson in the introduction to her book *Colour Me Beautiful*: "An Autumn person radiates in the warm, rich autumnal colours, with their golden undertones ... A Spring blossoms in clear, delicate colours and warm yellow undertones ... A Winter sparkles in the vivid, clear primary colours, and cool, icy colours ... And a Summer person glows in the pastels of June, the soft colours of the sea and sky, with their cool blue undertones." What this essentially means is that you will look good in some colours and not so good in others.

This system can also be applied to both jewellery and accessories. White metals harmonize with cool Winter and Summer colours, while gold tones work well with the warm shades of Autumn and Spring. You may not agree with this statement, but a way of testing a metal is to hold it against the palette of colours which suits you. The best jewellery for a Winter person is silver, platinum and white gold, diamonds, pearls with a white or grey cast, white ivory and white coral. A Summer person can use the same white metals as a Winter person, but may add rose gold, rose pearls and rose ivory. An Autumn person may wear gold, brass or copper tones, wooden jewellery, tortoiseshell and cream-coloured pearls. A Spring person also needs gold metals but must be careful to keep to delicate designs.

In addition to the colour, attention needs to be paid to the style of jewellery worn.

Do not draw attention to short stubby fingers by wearing large ornate rings. If you have a short neck, wear a necklace which falls below the base of the neck for a slimming effect. If, on the other hand, you have a long thin neck, you will look good in a choker which rests on the collarbone. Always try necklaces on when you buy them to make sure that they suit you. Necklaces made of more than one material, such as a mixture of gold and silver or gold and pearls, are more versatile.

Earrings make a woman look and feel 'dressed'. Choose earrings which complement the outfit you are wearing. Select triangular or sharp shapes with a tailored suit, but wear oval or round earrings with a softer, loosely structured garment. Avoid dangly earrings in the daytime as they are distracting; they also shorten the neck. Large earrings can have a softening effect on a short-haired woman and make her look less severe. In much the same way, a brooch worn on a lapel can make a woman look more feminine, simply because this is not a piece of jewellery worn by men. Brooches worn on the neck tend to make a woman look buttoned-up and perhaps a little straight-laced. For business, avoid wearing any jewellery which jangles (this particularly applies to bangles) as it will irritate you and your colleagues. Keep rings discreet unless you wish to look like a Christmas tree.

Having given all this careful thought, you are of course free to do your own thing and break all the rules. They are, after all, there to be broken.

A stunning piece of metallic cast-resin jewellery is shown off at its best on a low cut evening dress. The necklace is influenced by Egyptian motifs and the Key of Life hangs from the centre of the necklace. (*Left: Race Davies*)

Accessorizing jewellery

The choice of jewellery is highly individual as so much depends upon factors such as your budget, job, wardrobe and personality. One way of accessorizing jewellery is to aim for a specific effect.

• Theme your jewellery and accessories: whether its Art Nouveau, Art Deco, '50s retro, or Navaho (turquoise-and-silver Indian jewellery, a cowboy hat, a pair of tooled leather boots, leather belt and bandanna), stick with the details which have the same feel.
• Choose a signature category: be an earring person, or begin with brooches. The point is to choose a category you love and start collecting it.
• Let one piece of jewellery carry the look: wear an attention-grabbing item such as a giant brooch or perhaps a cluster of charms on a chain bracelet.
• Concentrate on lots of little things: try several slim chains worn together around your neck or a handful of distinctive rings.

Gallery

The work shown throughout this section of the book has been made by artists, craftspeople and jewellers, some of whom make jewellery exclusively, others whose artistic output is more general. The jewellery on these pages is purely inspirational, and I am not suggesting that as a beginner you will be able to achieve work of this quality immediately. Many of these artists have studied at art school and been making jewellery for years. However, having read this book and tried out many of the projects, you may feel you wish to take up jewellery-making as a serious hobby or even become a full-time jeweller.

Any aspect of the work shown may trigger off an idea. For example, you may like the shape or colour of a particular piece but not want to work in the same medium. There are no hard-and-fast rules saying that you should. Simply adapt the idea that has grabbed your attention, using the materials of your choice.

Although some of the jewellery here is made from expensive materials such as silver and gold, much of it is not. The joy of modern jewellery is that it does not have to be made from costly materials, so it is well within the reach of ordinary people. This means that people who otherwise might not be able to wear designer clothes can make their own individual style statement by wearing – and possibly making – designer jewellery.

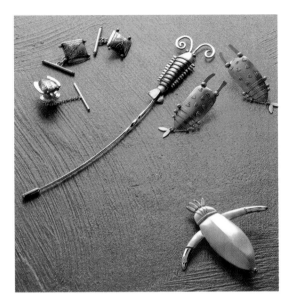

SARAH PARKER-EATON
Cuff links, hat pin, tie stud, earrings and brooch inspired by insects and fossils. The hat pin is made from oxidized silver with the addition of gold eyes. The cuff links at top left are made from oxidized silver with gold.
(*Above*)

KAREN WHITEROD
Articulated nylon jewellery – necklaces, bracelet and earrings. Note the way the light enhances the different colours, and the way the material naturally takes a spiral form.
(*Left*)

JESSICA TURRELL
Five brooches made from silver with slate and enamel finish. The pieces are very distinctive in style with a strong geometric, almost Art Deco influence. They are made from soft materials which need to be treated with care.
(*Opposite*)

TRISHA RAFFERTY
Made from porcelain often inlaid with precious metals, a collection of whimsical jewellery, including brooches, hat pins and earrings. Hearts, acrobats and fish are all recurring themes in this jeweller's work.
(*Left*)

HOLLY BELSHER
Necklaces made from silver tube and nine-carat gold-plate tube. Silver necklace made from cast units of shells, fish, etc. Gold-plate brooch and earrings from the 'Spiral' range; solid-silver necklace and earrings from the 'Shield' range.
(*Left*)

ANTHONY STERN
Better known for his hand-blown glass vessels, plates, jugs, goblets and vases, this artist occasionally makes strong pieces of jewellery like these. Often inspired by the sea or natural forms, they are highly sought-after and often adorn the front covers of fashion magazines.
(*Opposite*)

FOLDS OF LONDON
These origami butterfly, frog and peacock earrings are made from paper, which is then lacquered. Andrew Stoker, the man behind Folds of London, often uses marbled papers to create these tiny, intricate pieces of jewellery. Some pieces are also gilded with 24-carat gold leaf .
(*Left*)

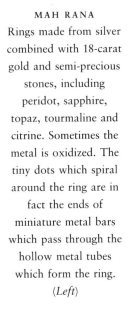

MAH RANA
Rings made from silver combined with 18-carat gold and semi-precious stones, including peridot, sapphire, topaz, tourmaline and citrine. Sometimes the metal is oxidized. The tiny dots which spiral around the ring are in fact the ends of miniature metal bars which pass through the hollow metal tubes which form the ring.
(*Left*)

ANNE FINLAY

Collection of necklace, brooches and earrings made from PVC (vinyl), nylon, laminates, rubber and stainless-steel wire. The shapes are cut from thick PVC and laminates using an engraving machine and sometimes a scalpel. Some of the PVC shapes are screen-printed with a texture or pattern. The pieces are assembled by drilling and gluing.
(*Right*)

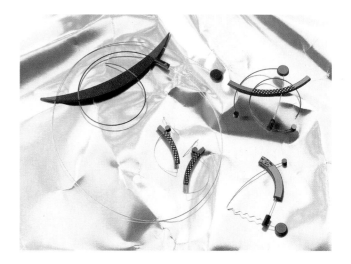

MANDY NASH

Jewellery from the 'Friendly Beasts' collection. Necklace known as Fulbert Fish, small fish earrings and brooches, all in reds, blues and pinks in anodized aluminium. At bottom left are dark blue Lettuce Lizard earrings; at bottom right, a green Cecil Chicken and a red Simon Snake.
(*Right*)

DEBBIE LONG
Necklaces, pendants and earrings made from silver and brass. The work is process- and material-led and is inspired by the metal and its inherent qualities. The metal is folded, forged and then opened up into three-dimensional forms.
Nothing is soldered.
(*Above*)

ROWENA PARK
These items of work, a brooch and drop earrings, were inspired by mutilated quartz. To achieve the effects, a combination of engraving, inlaying and painting have been used on clear acrylic.
(*Left*)

CREATING JEWELLERY

& ACCESSORIES

*J*ewellery-making has changed dramatically in the past few years, and designers have turned their attention from precious and costly jewellery to a glorious multitude of different materials, including papier mâché, wood, leather and textiles – all much more within the skill range and budget of the amateur. Easy-to-work metals, such as silver, copper and pewter, still have their place in the contemporary designer's repertoire, however, and there are simple techniques that can be used in the home with professional results. The following projects feature a wide range of stunning jewellery items and accompanying accessories, from rings, beads and necklaces, to earrings, brooches and hair slides, to make at home. Follow the instructions and photographs and you will find that creating these beautiful and exciting items is fun, affordable and achievable.

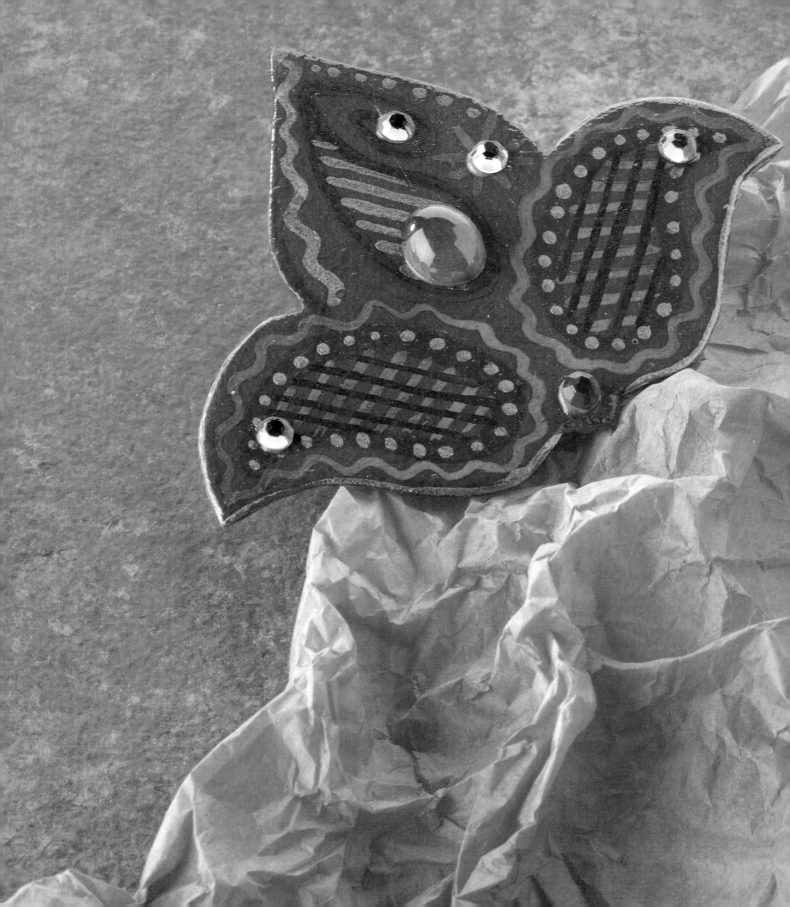

Hand-painted wooden brooch

This bold but pretty brooch is based on a fleur-de-lys shape and is decorated with a stylized paisley design. Although it looks complex, it is quite easy to follow. The same techniques can be applied to any basic shape and painting design, so experiment with your own ideas.

MATERIALS & EQUIPMENT

pen and paper
scissors
hobbyist plywood (¹⁄₁₆")
sandpaper
acrylic paints
paintbrushes
sponge
high-gloss acrylic varnish
diamanté
epoxy resin glue
brooch back

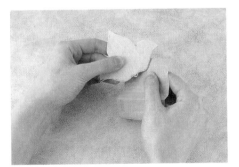

1 Draw the shape of the brooch on to paper, using the template at the back of the book as a guide, and cut it out to use as a template. Place the template on the hobbyist plywood and draw around it with a pen.

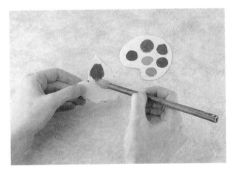

2 Cut out the plywood shape. Plywood is quite soft and you should be able to cut it out with a pair of scissors.

Plywood, a very thin wood ply, is ideal for jewellery-making as it is easy to cut and light to wear. Here, an exuberantly colourful brooch has been painted with acrylics and further decorated with flat-backed glass beads, or diamanté. The technique can be applied to earrings, too, with the addition of suitable earring findings. (*Opposite:* Annie Sherburne)

3 Smooth the cut edges of the shape with sandpaper to remove any burrs in the wood.

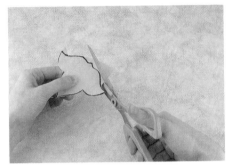

4 Paint the red base colour on the front of the brooch and leave to dry. Then paint the back of the brooch.

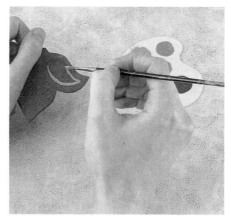

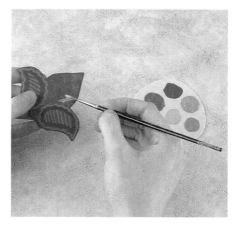

5 *Lightly sponge mauve on top of the base colour on both sides to create a mottled effect. Leave to dry.*

6 *Paint leaf-shaped outlines for the paisley design on the two lower 'petals' with yellow ochre. Leave to dry.*

7 *Add leaf-green stripes within the yellow ochre outlines, and then outline these with wiggly leaf-green lines. Add a green star to one side of the top 'petal'. Leave to dry.*

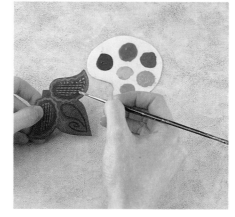

8 *With royal blue, add stripes to the yellow ochre outlines at right-angles to the green stripes. Paint a swirled leaf-shaped outline on the top 'petal'. Leave to dry.*

9 *Add gold dots, wiggles and stripes to finish the painted design. Leave to dry.*

10 *Seal both sides of the brooch with a high-gloss acrylic varnish and leave to harden. Stick on the diamanté with epoxy resin glue.*

11 Finally, stick on an appropriate brooch back with the same adhesive and leave to dry.

These plywood drop earrings have been decorated with felt-tip pens. The colours are divided by white and gold lines drawn with a paint pen. (*Right: Hammie Tappenden*)

These brooches and earrings are based on geometric shapes with a twist – a notch cut here and there. They are decorated in a distinctive style using acrylics and glass jewels. (*Above: Annie Sherburne*)

Papier mâché earrings

Papier mâché is a popular craft medium because the materials are inexpensive and easily available, and no special training or equipment is needed to get you started. Many artists/craftspeople who have trained in other disciplines have turned to papier mâché to produce wonderful bowls, boxes, sculpture and jewellery. Papier mâché jewellery can be almost any shape and size owing to the lightness of the material. It can be made from poster board on to which layers of papier mâché are added. It can also be formed over chicken wire, plastic or a balloon and can even be used over an old existing piece of jewellery which has outgrown its original purpose. Other materials such as shells, filler (as used to fill cracks in plaster walls), pieces of metal, gesso and pulped paper may be introduced into a piece.

MATERIALS & EQUIPMENT

wallpaper paste and a bowl for mixing

pencil and paper

poster board

scissors

newspaper

PVA (white) glue

white emulsion (latex) paint

paintbrushes

gouache paint in bright colours and black

acrylic varnish

2 earring backs

epoxy resin glue

PREPARATION
Mix the wallpaper paste with water in a bowl, following the manufacturer's instructions. Cover the work area with newspaper as papier mâché is messy. Make a space in an airing cupboard or somewhere warm to dry the piece between layers.

A bright and exuberant collection of papier mâché brooches and earrings. The simple shapes show off the strong black outline of the designs, which in turn enhance the bright colours. The earrings described in the step-by-steps are in the centre of the picture.
(Opposite: Anne-Marie Cadman)

1 Design the earrings on paper, indicating the colours you will use in the final piece. Draw the design on poster board, using the template at the back of the book as a guide, and cut out the shape to use as a template.

2 Draw around the template on to a piece of scrap poster board, then carefully cut out each earring. Cut a piece of newspaper the same shape as the earring but 1.5 cm (⅝ in) larger all around for the turnover.

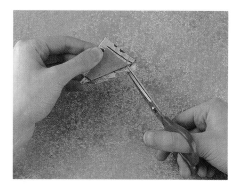

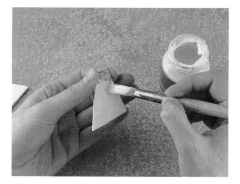

3 Stick the poster board triangle in the centre of the newspaper with PVA (white) glue and snip away the corners. Fringe the turnover, glue and press round on to the other side of the earrings to form a neat edge. Cover the exposed poster board with small pieces of newspaper and leave to dry. Repeat for the second earring.

4 When dry, cover each side of the earrings with two more layers of newspaper and leave to dry.

5 Apply two coats of white emulsion (latex) paint to the back and front of each earring, leaving them to dry between painting the front and back and each coat. Allow to dry.

6 Lightly draw the design on to the earrings in pencil. The pencil marks will not show through the painted decoration.

7 Paint the design on the fronts of the earrings using bright gouache colours. Two coats may be needed for an even, solid covering. Allow each colour and each coat to dry before painting the next.

8 Paint the black outline around the coloured areas using a fine paintbrush and add the black details. Leave to dry.

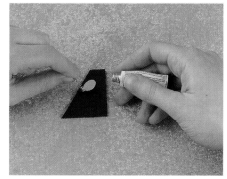

9 Paint the backs of the earrings black and leave to dry. You may need to apply two coats.

10 Using an acrylic varnish, apply one coat to the front and the edges of each earring. Leave to dry.

11 Glue on the earring backs using epoxy resin glue. Leave to harden before handling.

A collection of papier mâché earrings in a subtle range of colours and patterns, with different sections joined by jump rings. At bottom and right are a pair of papier mâché earrings and a brooch made using tissue paper. (*Right: tissue paper items, Gus Monro; others, Amanda Peach*)

Embossed paper cuff

Although made from paper, this wrist cuff is very sturdy and can be made even stronger by coating it with a solution of dilute PVA (white) glue when finished.

pencil and paper or poster board
pair of compasses or piece of string
scissors
thick watercolour paper
blue and green acrylic poster paints
PVA (white) glue
paintbrush
gold powder
knitting needle
fine-grade sandpaper
bradawl (awl)
paper fasteners

PREPARATION
To make the pattern, take your arm measurements and draw two parallel curves on to paper or poster board either with a compass or a piece of string and a pencil. Also draw five leaf shapes and five small circles. Cut out the shapes. Or, use the templates at the back of the book as a guide, and adapt to your measurements if necessary.

These three wrist cuffs are made from thick watercolour paper which is first painted then embossed. The distinctive decorative style is influenced by the designer's love of Indian and Celtic design. The cuff described in the project is on the right, together with matching earrings. The necklace is made of rolled-paper beads, threaded on to string and leather cord.
(Opposite: Gill Clement)

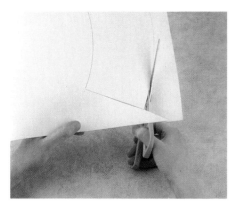

1 *Draw around the pattern pieces on to thick watercolour paper and cut out the shapes.*

2 *Mix green and blue acrylic poster paints with PVA (white) glue and paint on to the back of the cuff shape. The paint needs to be applied quite thickly – if you wish, use your fingers. Leave to dry.*

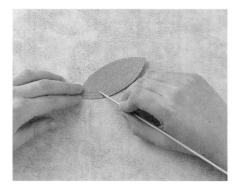

3 Paint the front of the cuff in the same way and dab on gold powder while the paint is still wet. Paint the circles with the greeny blue paint and dab on gold powder as you did on the cuff.

4 Coat the leaf shapes with PVA glue and then cover with gold powder. Using the knitting needle, emboss patterns into the leaf shapes and circles before the paint dries completely. When the paint is dry, sand off most of the gold colour from the circles using fine-grade sandpaper.

5 Glue the leaf shapes on to the cuff, spacing them evenly, and then glue the circles on to the centre of the leaf shapes. Using the knitting needle, emboss patterns over the exposed areas of the cuff.

6 Using fine-grade sandpaper, sand off most of the gold colour on the exposed areas of the cuff to reveal the gold embossed patterns.

7 Overlap the edges of the cuff and make matching holes with a bradawl (awl). Push through the paper fasteners and open out to secure the cuff.

A matching set of bangle, brooch and earrings feature a stark and effective monochrome design. Made from poster board papier mâché, the pieces are coated with white paint and decorated with black patterns made using a fine line pen. The panels of the bracelet are held together with shirring elastic.
(Opposite: Kate Smith)

Silk-painted hair slide

Silk painting is becoming very popular as a method of decorating cloth, and is used here to embellish a hair slide (barrette). A series of outlines is first painted on to the silk using metallic gutta before the colour is added. The gutta serves a practical purpose in that it prevents the silk paints from bleeding and merging into other areas of colour, but it is also a decorative feature in its own right, creating a glowing framework reminiscent of stained-glass leading.

MATERIALS & EQUIPMENT

heavyweight habotai silk
iron
hair-slide fitting (barrette)
black felt-tip pen
tracing paper
scissors
thick poster board
rubber-based glue (rubber cement)
wooden silk frame
silk pins or fine map pins
masking tape
vanishing textile marker
metallic gutta and applicator
silk paints in a variety of colours
paintbrushes
cotton buds (swabs)
white paper
thin foam rubber
fine braid
epoxy resin glue

PREPARATION

Wash, dry and press the silk. Protect the work surface with heavy plastic. Measure the hair-slide (barrette) fitting. The central design must be slightly longer than the fitting. Draw your chosen design in black felt-tip pen on the tracing paper, allowing a generous border all around the design for the turnover. Cut two pieces of thick poster board to the dimensions of the finished design, excluding the plain border. Stick the pieces of board together using a rubber-based glue (rubber cement) and leave to dry under a heavy object for approximately 24 hours.

The intricate design, inspired by Indian textiles and sari borders, the glowing colours, and the subtle sheen of silk, create a truly original hair accessory. The design and colours can be endlessly varied to complement any hair colour and outfit.
(Opposite: Sarbjit Natt)

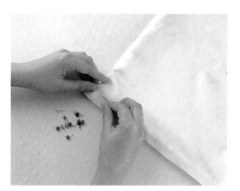

1 Stretch the silk on to the wooden frame and anchor it in position with the pins. The fabric must be absolutely taut with no wrinkles.

2 Place the traced design on top of the stretched silk and secure it in position with pieces of masking tape at each corner.

3   Turn the silk frame over and, using the vanishing textile marker, draw on the silk, following the design on the tracing paper below.

4   Turn the screen over again and remove the tracing paper. Apply the metallic gutta to the outlines of the design. This will block the mesh of the silk, preventing the silk paints from bleeding and merging in other areas of colour. Allow to dry completely.

5   Apply the silk paints. Small mistakes can be rectified by using a cotton bud (swab) dipped in water to lift off excess paint. Paint the plain border all around the design. Allow the fabric to dry before removing from the frame.

6   Place the painted silk face-down between two sheets of clean white paper. Iron, following the paint manufacturer's instructions, to fix the paints.

7   To assemble the hair slide, cut a piece of thin foam rubber a little larger than the board (see Preparation). Glue in place using rubber-based glue. Leave to dry for 30 minutes. Trim the edges of the foam to fit the poster board block.

8   Cut neatly around the silk design. Place the poster board block on the wrong side of the silk, with the foam against the fabric. Make sure that it is placed squarely on the central pattern. Apply rubber-based glue to the long sides of the block and stretch the silk firmly over it. Trim the silk at the corners and glue the short sides in the same way, making sure that the corners are neat. Leave to dry.

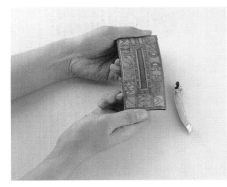

9 *Cut a piece of silk slightly smaller than the block and stick it on the back of the hair slide to cover the joins and neaten the edges. Trim the edges with fine braid to prevent fraying. Bend the block between the fingers and thumbs to shape it into a gentle arch which matches the shape of the hair-slide fitting. Glue the fitting to the back of the hair slide using epoxy resin glue, following the manufacturer's instructions carefully. Secure the fitting to the block with a piece of masking tape while the glue dries.*

*T*his beautiful collection of silk-painted hair slides (barrettes)and brooches are all made of habotai silk. The scarf at top left is decorated in the same way, but is made of silk chiffon which gives a delicacy to the painted design.
(*Above: Sarbjit Natt*)

Felt beads

These beads are made from that wonderful warm woolly material known as felt. You can either buy the fleece for making the felt ready-dyed, or dye your own. You can even make felt beads from pieces of fleece gathered from country hedgerows. The felting process involves wetting balls of tightly wound fleece in soapy water – the soap flakes speed up the process – and then massaging them with your hands. What you are effectively doing is shrinking the fleece and matting the fibres together.

These felt beads are made from brightly coloured fleece and have been strung together to make necklaces and a bracelet. Note the different shapes of bead, made by rolling and putting pressure on the ball in different ways during the felting process.
(Opposite: Victoria Brown)

MATERIALS & EQUIPMENT

fleece in various colours

soap flakes

bowl

craft knife

materials for decorating, including embroidery thread, stranded cotton, beads, sequins, expanding paints, etc

embroidery needle

silk thread

necklace finding (optional)

1 *Fleece can be dyed using domestic wool dyes, or bought ready-coloured in a range of vivid and subtle shades.*

2 *Sprinkle soap flakes into a bowl of warm water. To produce beads of a similar size, either weigh the fleece or measure it and form into equal-sized bundles. To make beads with a marbled centre, take a few strands of different colours of fleece and twist them together.*

3 *Cover the twisted multi-coloured fleece with fleece of one colour. Make this outside layer smooth. Roll into a ball shape.*

4 Dip the ball of fleece in the soapy water and squeeze the water through the ball. Holding your hands so that they cup the ball of fleece, roll the ball between your hands. Increase the pressure as you work.

5 Occasionally re-dip the ball in the water to make sure that there is plenty of soap in the centre of the ball. Keep rolling the ball and increase the pressure as you work to get the fibres inside moving.

6 The ball will gradually shrink. The longer you work the ball, the harder and smaller it will become as the fibres mat together. Allow 5–10 minutes per bead. Rinse out all the beads in clean unsoapy water.

7 To make a cone-shaped bead, shape the ball, while it is still soft, by pushing and pinching it towards its centre using your fingertips. Continue until the ball is hard.

8 To make a disc-shaped bead, flatten the soft ball between the palms of your hands and continue working until hard.

9 Leave the felt beads in a warm place to dry thoroughly. This may take a day or two.

10 Cut any marbled beads in half with a sharp craft knife to reveal the multi-coloured centres.

11 The beads can be left plain or decorated in various ways. For example, embroider stars on the beads using embroidery thread, stranded cotton or lurex.

12 Alternatively, sew sequins in place, each anchored with a rocaille bead. You can also use expanding paint to decorate beads.

13 To string a felt-bead necklace, use a large embroidery needle to thread the beads on to silk thread. Knot the ends or add a necklace clasp.

The sophisticated black necklace is decorated with pins glued into the beads. The red-and-black felt necklace and the hair-slide (barrette) are decorated with a discharge dye.
(*Right*: Victoria Brown)

*H*and-hooked earrings

These glittery earrings are made by hand-hooking materials on to a hessian (burlap) backing cloth, a textile technique which is usually associated with rag rugs. Although traditional materials such as cotton and wool can be used, these earrings have been made using strips of foil-backed sweet (candy) wrappers and crisp (chip) packets for a light-reflecting, densely textured finish. The effect is bright, modern and very individual.

*T*hese earrings, brooches and hair slide (barrette) are all made using the rag rug method of hand-hooking. The designer employs a variety of recycled materials and fabrics, including cotton, wool, nylon, jersey, felt, net, plastic and foil, to produce a multi-textural surface.
(Opposite: Lizzie Reakes)

MATERIALS & EQUIPMENT

pen

thin poster board

scissors

2 pieces of hessian (burlap), 30 cm (12 in) square

embroidery hoop, 15 cm (6 in) in diameter

permanent marker

foil-backed sweet (candy) wrappers or crisp (chip) packets

rag-rug hook

plastic spoon

latex carpet adhesive or PVA (white) glue

clear household cement

felt

cup-fastening earring backs

1 Draw a five-pointed or six-pointed star shape, with an approximate diameter of 6 cm (2½ in), on to poster board to create a template. Alternatively, use the template at the back of the book as a guide. Cut out the template.

2 Cut the hessian (burlap) to size and place in the embroidery hoop. Position the template in the middle of the hoop and draw around it using a permanent marker. Leave a good border between the star shape and the hoop to allow for working.

3 Cut the foil-backed wrappers and packets into 1 cm (1½ in) wide strips.

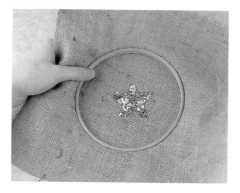

4 Take a strip of foil in one hand between your thumb and fore-finger and hold it loosely under the hessian; hold the hook in your other hand. To start, and working from the front, push the hook firmly through the hessian. Bring one end of the strip about 2.5 cm (1 in) up through the hole to the front. Push the hook in again, close to the first hole, and loop the foil on to the hook (the photograph above shows the rear view). Pull the loop through the hessian.

5 As you bring the loop through to the front, keep the tension taut and pull the foil back with the other hand until you have a small loop. Continue hooking from the centre outwards to create a looped pile about 3 mm (⅛ in) high. When you come to the end of the strip, bring the end up to the front and start again with a new strip as in step 4.

6 Remember to check the back of the hessian – it should look as neat as possible.

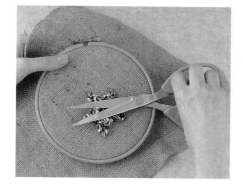

7 Finish filling in the star shape, remembering to hook all the ends to the front. Trim the ends level with the looped pile. Repeat to make the second star.

8 Using a plastic spoon, spread latex adhesive or PVA (white) glue all over the backs of the earrings, making sure they are well-covered. Leave to dry

9 Remove the hessian from the embroidery hoop. Cut around the star shape, leaving a good 1 cm (½ in) border for turning.

10 *Turn in the edges, snipping at intervals and pinching the edges together to create the shape. Allow to dry fully for two hours.*

11 *Apply a thin layer of strong multi-purpose glue to the reverse side and press it on to the felt backing.*

12 *Cut around the felt close to the star shape. Glue the cup fastening to the back with household cement and hold in position for 30 seconds. Leave to dry.*

*T*hese hand-hooked rings show a variation to the tightly hooked work seen in the main project. The flower effect is created by working the flower centres quite tightly and making the outer loops large and loose. The materials used are recycled plastic bags and crisp (chip) packets. (*Right: Lizzie Reakes*)

Machine-embroidered collar

Machine embroidery is becoming an extremely popular craft and is accessible to anyone with a modern sewing machine. The basic technique is seen applied to numerous objects, from jewellery and clothing to hats and boxes. This deceptively simple design, using just five colours, is based on a repeated snail motif, which was developed from the creation of spiral shapes which perfectly match the shape of a snail shell.

NOTE
If you are using a domestic sewing machine, the machine will need to rest every so often to stop the motor overheating. If machine embroidery is new to you, try practising on a spare piece of fabric to get the feel of the technique.

With machine embroidery the fabric is moved back and forth using an embroidery hoop, so there is no need to preset the stitch length. Hold the fabric taut in the embroidery hoop and work from the middle outwards. Practise and adjust the tension as necessary.

MATERIALS & EQUIPMENT

pencil and tracing paper
paper and coloured pencils
scissors
heavy unbleached cotton
embroidery hoop
sewing machine
coloured threads
iron
small piece of wadding (batting)
needle and dressmaking pins
fusible interfacing
backing fabric
two pearl buttons

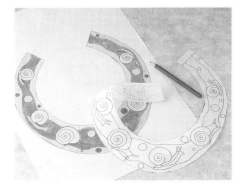

1   *Draw the shape of the collar on to tracing paper and plot out the design. When happy with the design, transfer it on to paper and experiment with different colour treatments. Alternatively, use the template at the back of the book as a guide. Add 1cm (½ in) to the template for seam allowances.*

2   *Using the coloured pattern as a guide, trace the outline of the design on to a piece of unbleached cotton with a pencil. If you cannot see the design beneath the cotton, tape it to a window so that the light shows up the pattern, or use a light box if you have one.*

This designer is better-known for her embroidered pictures but enjoyed the challenge of creating a piece of work to wear. This decorative collar is made using matt-coloured threads machine embroidered on to cotton. It does up at the back by means of small pearl buttons and hand-stitched button loops.
(Opposite: Helen Banzhaf)

3 Place the cotton in the embroidery hoop. To prepare the sewing machine, lower the teeth, remove the presser foot, set to straight stitch and the stitch length to zero. Keeping the cotton taut in the hoop, free machine embroider in sections, changing threads as necessary. Complete the collar in this way.

4 Press the fabric carefully on both sides and cut out the embroidered collar, leaving a 1 cm (½ in) border all around for turning.

5 Cut small pieces of wadding (batting) and hand-stitch them securely to the underside of the snail shells. This creates a three-dimensional effect on the right side of the work.

6 Cut the interfacing to the same size as the embroidery. Position the interfacing on the wrong side of the collar and iron to fuse.

7 Turn the 1 cm (½ in) border to the wrong side all around the collar. Snip at intervals for ease of turning and hand-stitch in place approximately 3 mm (⅛ in) from the turned edge.

8 Cut the backing fabric to the same size as the embroidery plus a 1 cm (½ in) allowance all around. Turn the allowance under to the wrong side and hand stitch in place, snipping at intervals so that the fabric lies flat.

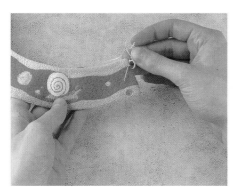

9   *Hand-stitch two button loops on the left-hand side of the collar. Make the loops a little larger than the buttons.*

10   *Hand-stitch the backing fabric to the underside of the collar, as neatly as possible.*

11   *Finally, attach two pearl buttons on the right-hand side of the collar, matching the position of the button loops.*

Machine-embroidered pin, earrings and brooches, embellished with small gold beads which complement the jewellery findings. Called 'Pageant Jewellery', the rich colours and geometric patterns are reminiscent of medieval heraldry designs. (Right : Janice Gilmore)

Polymer clay millefiori beads

Although one often sees enchanting brooches and beads made from polymer clay, it is very rare to find beads as finely decorated as the ones shown here. Reminiscent of the intricate millefiori Venetian glass beads, these clay beads are made using the same basic, and surprisingly simple, technique. Polymer clay can be purchased ready-coloured and is moulded while in its natural malleable state. The finished beads are then baked in a domestic oven to harden them.

This wonderful collection of earrings, brooches, necklace and individual millefiori clay beads reveals the myriad designs which can be achieved using this fascinating technique. (*Opposite*: *Deborah Alexander*)

MATERIALS & EQUIPMENT

polymer clay in various colours
marble rolling pin or straight-sided glass
craft knife
darning needle
2 eye pins
2 small gold-coloured beads
round-nosed pliers
2 earring findings

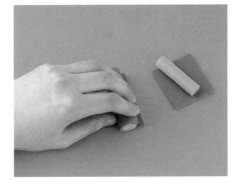

1 Millefiori canes are made from flattened sheets and rolled logs of polymer clay. Warm the clay and knead it so it is easy to work. Roll it out with a marble rolling pin or a straight-sided glass. The design detailed here is just one of hundreds of possible ideas. Adapt to make your own designs as wished.

2 To make the central cane, cut one rectangle of cerise clay and one, the same size, of blue clay. Place the cerise clay on top of the blue and, squeezing the ends over gently, roll the two pieces up together so it resembles a Swiss (jelly) roll. Do this as tightly and evenly as possible. Cut off a section and reserve for the tube beads in step 8.

3 To make the external canes, roll a long yellow log shape and cut a rectangular turquoise sheet. Wrap the yellow log in the turquoise sheet, making sure that the edges meet exactly. Roll the cane until it is long and thin, then cut into 6 pieces the same length as the central cane. Roll a thinner white cane and cut into 6 pieces.

4 Assemble the canes by positioning the turquoise/yellow canes alternately with the white ones evenly around the central cane. Gently squeeze the canes together.

5 Wrap the entire cane in a sheet of blue clay. Cut the edges to meet, then smooth them together. Gently roll the whole cane to consolidate all the elements. Make the cane longer and thinner by rolling with both hands on the table top.

6 The millefiori cane can be made as thin as you want - keep an eye on the pattern; if it gets too small the pattern may lose its clarity. If you wish, cut off a portion halfway through rolling to use as a design element on other beads. Cut thin slices from the cane with a craft knife.

7 Make a ball from scraps of clay and cover with slices from the millefiori cane. Either cover the bead completely or place pieces intermittently over it. Repeat to make a second identical ball.

8 Roll the balls between your palms to fuse the pieces together. Make two tube-shaped beads, using the reserved piece of blue and cerise cane (see step 2). Roll the cane until quite thin, then cut into two sections and decorate with the millefiori slices. Square beads can be made in the same way, this time flattening the sides of the log before cutting into sections.

9 Pierce the balls and tubes with a darning needle, first from one side, then from the other – this prevents the shapes from distorting. Bake all the beads in the oven, following the clay manufacturer's instructions for oven temperature and baking time.

10 To assemble the earrings, take an eye pin and thread a tube, a small gold bead and a round millefiori bead on to it. Using round-nosed pliers, turn the remaining wire to form a loop (to stop beads falling off). Repeat with the other eye pin and beads.

11 Take the earring findings and open the fish-hook loops at one end by turning them sideways. Slide them on to the eye pins, then close the hooks to secure.

*I*n complete contrast in style and technique to the polymer clay beads, these earrings and brooch are made from the same material, cut and moulded into shape. Decorated with gold paint, and inlaid with faceted and plain glass stones, they are immensely eye-catching.
(*Right: Lushlobes*)

Leather 'seaweed' necklace

This beautiful organic necklace is made from soft, tanned leather which is punched, moulded, dyed and twisted into shapes to resemble seaweed washed up on to the seashore.

MATERIALS & EQUIPMENT

25 leather cords, 90 cm (36 in) long by 30 mm (⅛ in) wide

natural-coloured, vegetable-tanned hide

pen and poster board

scissors

leather punch

cutting board or mat

art knife and blades

leather tool or knitting needle

leather glue

press stud or similar object

yellow and brown leather dyes

rubber gloves

household brush

1   *Using the templates at the back of the book as a guide, draw the following on to poster board: front and back for two fish A; front and back for one fish B; two centres for fish A; one centre for fish B; one large seaweed leaf; one small seaweed leaf; and one seaweed band. Cut out the templates and draw around them on the flesh side of the leather.*

2   *Cut out the fish and seaweed using scissors. Make the holes marked on the seaweed templates with a leather punch.*

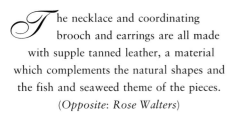

The necklace and coordinating brooch and earrings are all made with supple tanned leather, a material which complements the natural shapes and the fish and seaweed theme of the pieces.
(Opposite: Rose Walters)

3   *Using an art knife, carefully shave the edges of the fish, the fish centres and the three seaweeds to thin out the leather.*

4   *Dampen the fish shapes with water and then mark the pattern on the body using a leather tool or a knitting needle. Mark lines on the fins.*

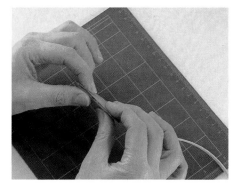

5 Gently mark, but do not cut out, the eyes on the fish pieces using the leather punch.

6 To assemble a fish, coat the wrong sides of both the back and front pieces with leather glue. Place a corresponding centre piece and a cord on the front piece, as shown.

7 Stick together the two halves of the fish, sandwiching the centre piece and tail. Pay particular attention to the edges so that they are neat. Repeat with the remaining fish.

8 To shape the seaweed, dampen the pieces with water and twist the seaweed leaves. Draw central lines on to the seaweed band and then mould dimples by pressing on to a stud or similar object.

9 Wearing rubber gloves, dye some of the items and cords yellow and others brown. Do this while the pieces are still wet for a natural, uneven colouring. If you want a mottled effect, dab the dye randomly on to the leather.

10 When the leather pieces and cords are dry, polish all the items with a household brush.

11 To assemble the necklace, take 18 cords and line them up, then tie a knot in the middle.

12 Tie the seaweed leaves on to one cord on the left-hand side. Tie the fish on to the right-hand side.

13 Twist the seaweed band and secure by threading a cord through it. Slot it on to the necklace above the fish.

14 Overlap the cords at the top of the necklace and bind together with the remaining cord.

*T*his collection of leather jewellery features another natural theme, this time of leaves. The necklace is made of ivy leaves, which overlap each other imitating the growing habit of ivy. Two pairs of leaf earrings, one undyed leather, the other stained brown, and a leaf brooch complete the collection.

(Right: Rose Walters)

Hand-strung necklace

This lovely necklace is made from specially-made enamelled beads and semi-precious stones including fluorspar (fluorite), crystal, amethyst, onyx, blue agate, silver, malachite, sodalite and glass. The knotting between each bead makes the necklace longer and becomes part of the design as well as strengthening the necklace. Match the fastening to the colour of the beads.

MATERIALS & EQUIPMENT

beads of your choice

coloured nylon threads

bubble wrap or a piece of fabric on which to lay the beads while working

plasticine

scissors

5-amp fuse wire

gimp (a fine hollow metallic thread)

flat-nosed pliers

jewellery findings

fine tweezers

matches

NOTE
When choosing threads for stringing necklaces, select them in colours which complement the beads so that they become part of the overall design. You will see the knots between the beads, and the threads will also be visible through transparent beads. The number of strands you will need depends on the weight of the necklace.

1 String the beads temporarily on to nylon thread to get the feel of how the necklace will hang and how the beads work together in colour and shape. Try it on for size, bearing in mind that knotting will add an extra 1 cm (½ in) to the finished length. Remember also to take the clasp into consideration. The necklace should be at least 40 cm (16 in) long.

2 Place the bubble wrap or fabric on the work top (this is to stop the beads from rolling around). Make a necklace-shaped sausage from plasticine. Note that the beads at either end of the necklace should have larger holes as the thread will go through them twice. Take the beads off the temporary thread and place them in order on the plasticine.

Necklace of semi-precious stones and enamelled pieces, knotted between components. The charm of the piece lies in the melange of soft colours within the stones; the stunning enamelled beads are hand-crafted by the maker. The earrings are made of enamelled and tourmaline beads.
(Opposite:
Alexandra Raphael)

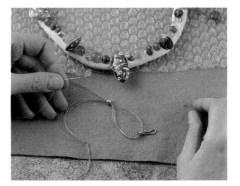

3   Cut two strands of thread; they will be used doubled so always cut much more thread than you think necessary. Cut a 10 cm (4 in) piece of 5-amp fuse wire and fold it in half, halfway down the threads, to make a needle. Twist the wire so the needle does not come apart. Knot the four thread ends together.

4   Cut a 1 cm (½ in) piece of gimp. Trim the needle to a point. Remember that the first bead you thread will be the last in the necklace. Thread the bead on to the needle and push it to the end. Put the gimp on next – hold the needle with flat-nosed pliers and use the other hand to manoeuvre the gimp and slide it over the thread all the way down to the first bead.

5   Put a catch on the thread next, then take the needle back through the first bead. Do not pull the loop tight.

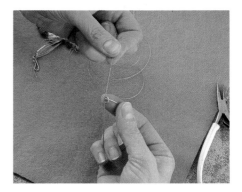

6   Thread the rest of the beads in the correct order in the same way. After the last bead, thread on the jump ring and then a 1 cm (½ in) piece of gimp.

7   Remove the needle from the threads. Take the loop of threads in one hand and thread the entire necklace through the loop, keeping the gimp and the jump ring separate.

8   Once the necklace is through, slide the gimp to the end of the loop with the jump ring.

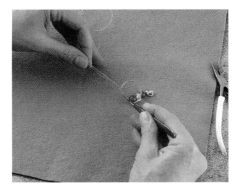

9 Pull the threads to close the loop. The jump ring is now suspended from the doubled-up gimp.

10 Start knotting. Pull each bead to the end in turn and tie a regular knot. Hold the thread tight against the bead with tweezers to get the knot as close and tight as possible.

11 To tighten, pull two threads in each hand. Gently pull the next bead along.

12 Continue knotting by pushing the necklace through the loop of threads and knotting until just before the last bead.

13 Pull the slack so that the gimp is up against the last bead. Pull the thread gently through the last bead to tighten. Trim the excess thread to about 10 cm (4 in).

14 Tie a half-hitch knot between the last and next to last bead. To tighten, pull two threads in each hand. Separate the two threads and pull round and tie an over-hand knot. Cut the thread close to the last bead, about 5 mm (¼ in). Strike a match and melt the ends of the thread until they shrink to almost nothing.

Cast-resin earrings

Although cast-resin jewellery looks difficult to make, it is in fact a straightforward process and the results look so good that it is well worth trying. You do not even have to be good at modelling as you can cast from found objects, such as the shell- and sea-horse-shaped chocolates used here.

MATERIALS & EQUIPMENT

chocolates or other objects to cast
sharp knife or craft knife
acrylic varnish
old paintbrushes
rubber-based glue (rubber cement)
non-porous plastic container
rubber latex
resin and hardener
aluminium filler, for metallic finish (optional)
plastic container and spatula
matchstick
coarse sandpaper
fine wet-and-dry paper
metal polish and soft cloth
pendant drill
2 beads
2 short lengths of gold-coloured wire
round-nosed pliers
2 earring backs
household cement

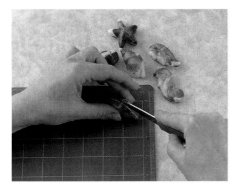

1 If the chocolate shapes you are using are moulded on both sides, cut them in half. Try to do this with cold hands to prevent the chocolate melting.

2 Varnish the found or made object to achieve a smooth finish. Porous materials, such as wood or, as in this case, chocolate, may need two or three coats of varnish. Remember to allow each coat to dry thoroughly before applying the next.

3 Stick your objects with rubber based glue (rubber cement) flat-side down in the plastic container. Mix the rubber compound following the manufacturer's instructions. Using an old paintbrush, lightly coat the objects with rubber, working the compound into any indentations to avoid air bubbles.

The finished earrings, seen here with a matching necklace, are a lovely burnished silver-grey colour, which is due to the aluminium filler mixed with the resin. The shapes are bold yet detailed, and give an impression of substance although cast-resin jewellery is surprisingly light to wear.
(Opposite: Race Davies)

4 Pour the remaining rubber into the container, making sure that all the objects are covered. Leave to set. Remove the rubber mould from the container and take out the objects. You will probably find that some of the compound has seeped under the edges of the objects. Trim away the excess rubber with a craft knife.

5 Mix up the resin and add the hardener and the aluminium filler (if using), following the manufacturer's instructions. Use a plastic container with a spout, if possible, so that the resin is easier to pour. There are many coloured pigments available to add to resin, including transparent, as well as various metallic finishes.

6 Pour in just enough resin to fill the moulds. With complicated shapes it is advisable to work the resin into the mould with a matchstick.

7 Once the resin has set hard it can be removed from the moulds. Try to touch the shapes as little as possible as the top surface may still be slightly tacky. Leave the shapes for a few hours to harden properly.

8 Smooth the shapes, first using a coarse sandpaper and then fine wet-and-dry paper. Polish with metal polish and a soft cloth if using a metallic filler.

9 Using a pendant drill or a drill with a very fine bit, drill holes for the wire and bead attachment separating the two cast shapes which form the earring.

10 To assemble an earring, thread one end of a wire through one of the cast shapes and bend the end round with round-nosed pliers to secure. Thread on a bead, then pass the wire into the other cast shape and bend to secure.

11 Stick the earring backs on to the reverse sides of the earrings using household cement.

These cast-resin necklaces and earrings are made in the same way as detailed in the project, but using moulds hand-carved from soft wood. The theme is Egyptian, and the pieces have bronze and copper finishes (*Right*: *Race Davies*)

Repoussé pewter brooch

Although encompassing traditional jewellery techniques, including repoussé, sawing and soldering, this brooch is in fact fairly easy to make if you take one step at a time.

NOTE
Always wear a face-mask and protective gloves when soldering, and work in a well-ventilated room. Keep all dangerous substances well away from children.

1 Design the brooch on paper and cut out a template in poster board, or use the template at the back of the book as a guide. Lay the template on the pewter and score around it with a

2 Carefully follow the scribed outlines and cut out the bird-like shape using tin snips.

3 Place the brooch face-down on the block, which can be made of metal, wood or pitch. Hold the ball-shaped punch tool on the metal and strike it with the flat end of the hammer. Make two dome shapes in the metal, one larger than the other.

MATERIALS & EQUIPMENT

pen and paper

poster board

scissors

sheet of pewter

scriber

tin snips

block and repoussé tools (ball-shaped punch and pattern tool)

hammer

bench peg and C-clamp

drill

piercing saw with 1.5 mm (1/16 in) blade

scraper

sheet of brass

steel wool

face-mask and protective gloves

heat source, such as a fine-nozzled blowtorch

solder and flux

epoxy resin glue

glass stones with flat backs

brooch back

metal polish

Bird-like in character and with a lovely surface texture, this brooch is made from pewter – an ideal metal for beginners as it is soft and malleable. Set into the metal are two glowing glass beads.
(Opposite: Heini Philipp)

4 Punch a decorative pattern into the outer edge of the metal with the pattern tool. Repeat on the other side.

5 Using the bench peg and C-clamp to support the brooch, and with the brooch face-down, drill two guide holes for the stone settings. Thread the piercing saw through the guide hole, then saw a hole large enough to hold the stone, with a 1 mm ($\frac{1}{16}$ in) edge overlap all around. Repeat for the second stone setting.

6 Still with the brooch face-down, scrape around the holes with a scraper to make concave shapes to accept the stones.

7 Scribe around the formed shape on to the sheet of brass to make a backing plate the same size. Cut out the brass with tin snips, and rub with steel wool to smooth any rough edges.

8 Wearing a face-mask and protective gloves, solder the brooch back on to the back of the brass plate. To do this, apply the flux to the back of the brass and heat it from underneath to make the solder flow.

9 Place the brooch front over the brass backing plate and scribe through the holes to mark the places where the stones will fit.

10 *Using epoxy resin glue, stick the stones into place on the right side of the brass plate. Then stick the back of the pewter brooch to the front of the brass plate. To finish, clean with metal polish.*

Dazzling Celtic-style pewter necklace, with coordinating earrings and heart-shaped brooch. All the pieces are decorated with patterns marked from the back of the metal and coloured stones.
(Opposite: Gill Clement)

Paper & copper necklace

This very effective jewellery is made from a combination of hand-made and dyed papers, copper wire and sheet copper. Although the process involves metalwork, it does not require specialist skills. You can make jewellery to go with many different outfits by altering the coloured paper used.

MATERIALS & EQUIPMENT

pen and poster board

scissors

waterproof pen (permanent marker)

soft copper foil 15 cm (6 in) wide, 008 thall (thickness)

fine tin snips (optional)

cutting board or mat

bradawl or drill with a fine bit

tack hammer and small anvil

small pliers

camping gas burner

cotton wool

methylated spirits (denatured alcohol)

PVA (white) glue

hand-made, natural or recycled papers

skewer

jump rings

necklace fastener

1 *Draw the jewellery shapes on poster board. Cut out the templates and use to mark out the pieces on the metal with a waterproof pen (permanent marker). Or, use the templates at the back of the book as a guide. Here, spare copper shapes are being used as templates.*

2 *Cut out all the copper pieces with scissors or fine tin snips.*

3 *On a cutting board or mat, make holes in the top corners as marked on the templates, using either a bradawl or a drill fitted with a fine bit.*

*B*right, original and surprisingly easy to make, this necklace is formed from triangles of copper, which reduce in size towards the fastening, overlaid with hand-made papers. Complete with matching pin brooch and earrings. (*Opposite: Deirdre Hawken*)

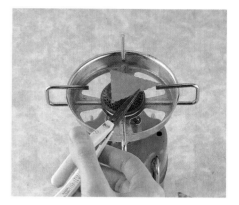

4 Using scissors, carefully cut the undulating curves into the sides of the shapes.

5 Smooth and flatten the edges with a tack hammer on a small anvil to avoid sharp edges.

6 Hold each shape with pliers, and patinate the metal over the flame of a gas burner until it discolours. This usually takes less than a minute. Dampen a piece of cotton wool with methylated spirits (denatured alcohol) and wipe over the metal to clean it.

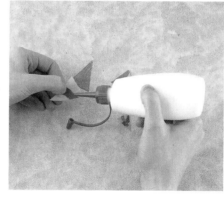

7 Dilute some PVA (white) glue half and half with water and use to paint the sheets of paper to strengthen them. Allow to dry, then cut out triangular pieces of paper and rip and cut smaller abstract shapes.

8 Overlay the ripped shapes on top of the paper triangles and stick them together with PVA glue. Leave them to dry.

9 Hold a skewer in the burner flame until hot, then touch the edges of the paper to give a burnt edge. Make holes over the surface of the paper in the same way.

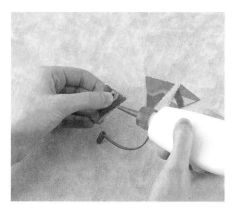

11 Lay the triangles out starting with the largest in the centre and arranging the graduated sizes evenly on either side. Use jump rings and pliers to connect the triangles together, and add a necklace fastener to complete the necklace.

10 Stick the paper triangles on to the copper with white glue and leave to dry.

These pieces are made in the same way as the project necklace, but employ a more muted colour treatment. An additional layer, of tooled and pattern copper, has been added to each piece.
(*Above: Deirdre Hawken*)

$\mathscr{S}$ilver-wire rings

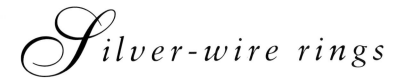

This fine, intricately coiled ring is made from silver-nickel wire and is adorned with one ceramic bead and one of dyed horn. To make it you will need some specialist equipment, and the process involves heating the wire to make it malleable. Do take great care when working over the flame, and also when using the dilute sulphuric acid, and follow the instructions given here to the letter.

$\mathscr{A}$ very simple way of creating stylish rings is to twist wire around a mandrel and then spiral it around semi-precious stones, beads or bone. These rings, made with silver-nickel and copper wire, are bold and need large hands to carry them off to best advantage. The ring described in the project is at bottom left.
(*Opposite: Heini Philipp*)

NOTE
When diluting sulphuric acid, wear protective rubber gloves and always add the acid to the water, not the other way round. Alternatively, use alum (see Basic techniques, page 117). For a homemade pickle, use a solution of 1 dessertspoon salt in 250 ml (8 fl oz) malt vinegar. Leave the metal in the solution for an hour.

MATERIALS & EQUIPMENT

mandrel and vice
2 mm ($\frac{1}{12}$ in) silver-nickel wire, about 38 cm (15 in) long
flat-nosed pliers
gas canister and portable burner
rubber gloves
dilute sulphuric acid (1 part acid to 8 parts water)
2 beads
hammer and block
wire cutters
metal file

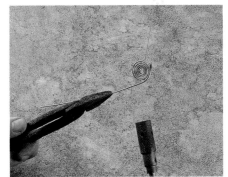

1   Clamp the mandrel into the vice and twist the wire, about 7.5 cm (3 in) from one end, around it to form a ring shape.

2   Remove the wire from the mandrel. Coil the longer end of the wire around itself, about five times, to form a disc shape on top of the ring.

3   The metal must be annealed – or tempered – to make it malleable and easy to work. To do this, grip the half-made ring between pliers and heat it over a gas burner until the metal becomes discoloured.

4 *Wearing protective rubber gloves, dip the ring into dilute sulphuric acid to clean off the oxide. Wash off the acid under running water.*

5 *Push the longer end of the wire up through the centre of the coil and pull it tight with a pair of flat-nosed pliers.*

6 *Thread on a bead so that it rests flat on top of the coil. Coil the long end of wire around itself, about two times.*

7 *Forge – or beat – the wire with a hammer on a block to flatten it and to harden the wire. Pull the wire coils up and down around the bead to enclose it. Cut the ends of the wire to 1 cm (½ in) at each end.*

8 *Bend the ends of the wires so that they are pointing towards each other, then file them flat so that both pieces will fit into the last bead.*

9 *Fit the last bead on to the side of the ring, and then push the wire down firmly to hold the bead securely in position.*

These armbands are made from various metals including silver. They are masculine pieces of decoration, miniature versions of which would make wonderful rings.
(Opposite: Heini Philipp)

*G*lass brooch

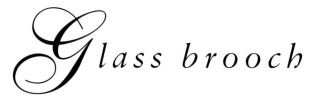

Jewellery made from glass has wonderful light-reflecting properties – it is literally dazzling. The brooch described here is made from broken rose and purple opaque glass, transparent turquoise glass, buttons and tiny beads. The process involves soldering, so you will need a soldering iron. Always use a soldering iron with care, following the manufacturer's instructions, and wear a face-mask and protective gloves.

MATERIALS & EQUIPMENT

buttons in various sizes
White glue
tiny beads
goggles
glass in various colours
round-nosed pliers
white cloth/paper
sticky-backed copper foil,
2 mm (³⁄₁₆ in), 3 mm (⁷⁄₃₂ in),
4 mm (¼ in), and 5 mm (³⁄₈ in) widths
75-watt soldering iron and stand
water-soluble flux crystals
small paintbrush
face-mask
solder
protective gloves
sal ammoniac (chemical compound)
brooch back
small brush
metal file
glass cleaner or furniture polish

1 Place the large button on a flat surface and stick the smaller button in the centre with white glue.

2 Glue the tiny beads around the edge of the smaller button with the same adhesive.

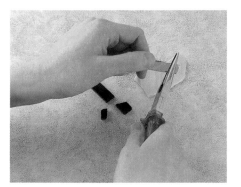

3 Wearing goggles, start to shape the coloured/textured glass. Use flat-nosed pliers to break the glass into small pieces carefully and slowly. Cut the coloured glass over white cloth or paper so you can see the pieces easily.

*T*hese brooches are made from broken opaque and transparent glass pieces, mirror glass, beads, buttons and shell. The pieces are wrapped in copper foil and then carefully soldered together. The brooch described in the project is at the centre left.
(Opposite: Rachel Maidens)

4 After the glass has been shaped, apply the sticky-backed copper foil all around the edge of the glass pieces and button. Press down firmly to secure in place.

5 Turn on the soldering iron to begin warming up for at least 5 minutes and then switch off until it is ready to use again. When the copper foil is secure, apply flux crystals (diluted with water) with a small paintbrush. Make sure that all the copper foil has been coated with flux otherwise the solder will not stick to the surface.

6 Now place the design on a flat surface, away from the white cloth/paper. Turn on the soldering iron and leave to heat up for 5 minutes. Put on the goggles and face-mask (the fumes from the soldering iron are dangerous). Melt a piece of solder on to the soldering iron, then apply drops of solder between the pieces which lie side by side around the brooch. You may need to wear protective gloves as the metals can become very hot.

NOTE
The soldering iron must be turned off after 15–20 minutes otherwise it will become too hot and will not melt the solder properly. When it is turned off, it must be left to cool for a few seconds. Sal ammoniac (a chemical compound) should then be applied to clean off any solder left on the tip.

7 Take the soldering iron slowly over the small drops of solder so that they melt evenly over the pieces.

8 Repeat the soldering on the other side of the brooch, brushing over with more flux before applying the solder.

10 Leave to cool on a flat surface, then place in warm water and leave for 5 – 10 minutes. Using a small brush, brush over the front and back of the brooch to remove any solution and use a metal file to remove any solder still remaining on the brooch. Dry by placing on a clean cloth or towel and leave to dry. Polish with glass cleaner or furniture polish.

9 Take a short piece of copper foil and place it on the inside of the brooch back. Brush over with flux and then apply plenty of solder so that it secures the fastener to the brooch.

*T*his range of jewellery is created with both men and women in mind and includes cuff links, a tie pin, a necklace, a brooch and earrings in matt silver. Individual elements are soldered into place using silver solder and flux. (*Right*: Stephen Anderson)

EMBELLISHMENTS
& ACCESSORIES

Decorative accessories are wonderful style statements and, mixed-and-matched with care, will transform your wardrobe and offer a new look with very little outlay. This section of the book is full of varied ideas for making and choosing a wide range of delightful accessories, from machine-embroidered hat pins and beaded hair combs, to buttons covered in marbled silk and glittery bow trims. There are also creative suggestions for embellishing clothing, hats, shoes and bags, with appliquéd trims, machine embroidery, woven button trims and removable button covers. There are fun ideas for simple jewellery items too, including a brightly decorated bead necklace that children can make, quick-to-crochet raffia earrings and an inventive range of jewellery made from recycled Christmas decorations. With simple step-by-step sequences to follow, you will see how easy it is to embellish your wardrobe and enliven your look with individual accessories.

Hat pins & pin brooches

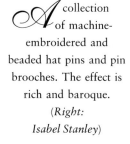

A collection of machine-embroidered and beaded hat pins and pin brooches. The effect is rich and baroque.
(Right: Isabel Stanley)

Hat pins have taken on a new lease of life in recent years due to the soaring popularity of hats - more and more people are now choosing hats for everyday wear and not just for formal occasions. Almost any-

thing can be attached to a hat pin and, as long as you have a pin with a safety cover for the tip, the pin can be worn in a hat or as a brooch. Some lovely examples of both approaches are shown here, but if you want to make something very quick and easy, try the following idea. Thread some decorative beads on to a hat pin and add a crimping bead after the last bead. Squeeze the crimping bead with pliers until the two sides come together and close so it holds the rest of the beads on the pin.

Embroidered Hat pin

MATERIALS & EQUIPMENT

sheet of brass
tin snips
metal file
3 brass hat pins, 15 cm (6 in) long
round-nosed pliers
round-nosed hammer and anvil
wire-cutters
epoxy resin glue
silk fabric scraps and sequin waste
cotton, lustre, and fine and thick gold threads
hot-water-soluble fabric
PVC (vinyl) transparent plastic
sewing machine
embroidery hoop
beads

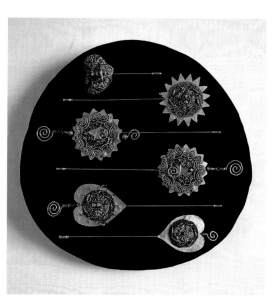

These highly textural and intricate hat pins are made from cut metal decorated with free machine-embroidery, using a variety of plain, lustre and gold threads.
(Right: Judy Clayton)

1 Cut out your chosen base shape from the brass with tin snips, and also a 4 x 1 cm (1½ x ½ in) rectangle and a triangle with sides 1 cm (½ in) long. File the edges smooth. Hammer the base shape and triangle on both sides until they are covered with textured bumps.

2 Bend a spiral at one end of two hat pins with the pliers, then beat the spirals flat. Position on the base, bend a right-angle on both wires where they meet and then trim the waste. Make a smaller spiral for the triangle. Glue the spirals in position on the base back and cover the joins with the rectangle.

3 Sandwich the silk scraps, sequin waste and some bright threads between the soluble fabric and the PVC (vinyl), with the PVC on top. Stitch the sandwich together with free machine stitching. Use the darning foot down and have the teeth down so you can move the embroidery freely. Turn the piece upside down and stitch again, varying the threads, in a loose pattern. Cut out a circular piece.

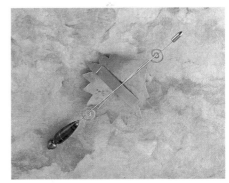

4 Stretch some soluble fabric in the hoop and place the circle on top. Decrease the spool tension so the lower thread will be visible on the top surface. Using contrasting threads, stitch around the edge and pattern around the circle.

5 Cut out the embroidered piece, pour boiling water over it and leave to dry. Push the back wire of the metallic triangle through to the back of the embroidery. Roughen the front surface of the base shape and glue the embroidery on to it.

6 Thread and glue the beads on to the hat pin. Pass the pin through the spirals, as shown, to anchor.

Hair accessories

*T*his collection of hair accessories features a variety of materials and different techniques. Felt-bead slide (barrette) and bobbles (Victoria Brown); appliquéd-hearts slide (Abigail Mill); painted-wood slide (Hammie Tappenden); glass slide (Gaynor Ringland); beaded slides (Janet Coles Beads). (*Below*)

A hair accessory may be as simple as a hair band wound with ribbon to match a dress, or as elaborate as an intricately beaded hair comb. Many of the other jewellery techniques shown in this book may be used to make hair slides (barrettes), such as a hand-hooked hair slide or bobbles made from felt beads tied on to elastic. If you are marbling fabric (see page 93), allow a little extra fabric to make a hair scrunch (simply a piece of fabric sewn around a short length of cord elastic).

To make the ornate combs we have decorated here, buy metal or plastic hair combs from a bead shop. The easiest way to decorate a comb with beads is to cover the top of the comb with fine, stretchy meshed fabric – corset elastic is ideal and is available from fabric stores in basic colours. Netting or ordinary elastic or Lycra can be used instead. This provides a base on which to sew the beads.

Another way to decorate a comb is to thread beads on to thin wire and arrange them in a pattern at the front of the comb: use blue rocailles and bugles on a red comb, for instance. Alternatively, glue mounted diamanté beads to the comb.

A lovely glittery scarf is used here as a pony-tail tie by twisting it around the hair. (*Above: Susie Freeman*)

Beaded *Hair comb*

These three hair combs have been decorated with beads and sequins to produce very different effects: one has sophisticated black and white beads sewn on in ordered rows; one uses gold coins with small gold rocailles for an exotic finish; while the third version is decorated with silver shell sequins and glass beads for a more youthful look.
(*Left: Karen Triffitt*)

MATERIALS & EQUIPMENT

corset elastic, netting or Lycra
hair comb
needle, thread and scissors
small beads

1 Fold a piece of corset elastic over the top of the comb and sew into place through the prongs.

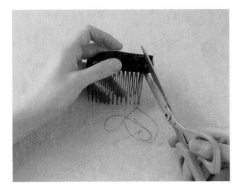

2 Cut the sides of the elastic to the shape of the comb, leaving just a minimal overlap.

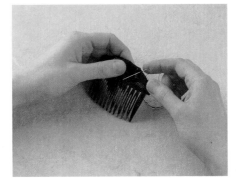

3 Oversew the cut edges with matching thread so that the elastic fits tightly but is not stretched.

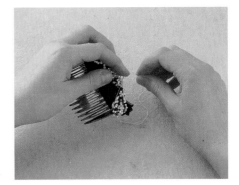

4 Sew bugle beads, rocailles, and small glass and plastic shapes on to the elastic until it is covered.

Buttons & bows

Buttons can make or break a garment, which is why it is small details such as these that are so important. Buttons which can be covered with a fabric of your choice are available from good haberdashery departments, or you can buy button covers, decorated in all manner of fun or sophisticated ways, to change the look of an outfit temporarily. Alternatively, buy the basic button covers and decorate them yourself with beads, bottle tops or found objects to match favourite outfits. Look out for antique and period buttons in auctions and second-hand shops. Bows can be bought ready-made, but it is easy to make your own to attach to garments and accessories as an immediate embellishment.

Buttons with a difference in coils, hearts, squares, circles and lipped shapes. Some are self-coloured, others are inlaid with metal, and all are made from porcelain.
(Below: Trisha Rafferty)

These wonderful glittery bows are made from machine-knitted fabric containing a variety of elements from beads, sequins and glitter fabric.
(Above: Susie Freeman)

MATERIALS & EQUIPMENT

marbling kit consisting of thickening powder and marbling colours
distilled water
marbling bath – a photographic developing tray, for example
eye dropper or pipette
paintbrush or comb
fine silk fabric, pre-washed and ironed
iron

Marbling *Silk*

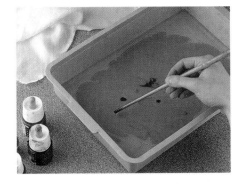

1 Mix one heaped teaspoon of the thickening powder with 1 litre (1¾ pints) distilled water and leave to stand for at least 1 hour. Pour the mixture into the marbling bath to a depth of 4–5 cm (1½–2 in).

2 Using an eye dropper or pipette, drop the chosen colours on to the surface of the mixture. The colours will float on the surface and spread out slowly from the centre. Add drops of the second and third colours in the same way.

3 When the surface is full of colour, make patterns by swirling the paint around. You can use the end of a paintbrush or a comb for this.

4 Carefully ease the fabric on to the medium. Lift off the cloth vertically so the pattern is not disturbed. Holding it by the corners, rinse under cool running water until it no longer feels slippery. Hang it up to dry, then iron on the back to fix the colours.

*M*arbled silk can be used in numerous ways. The buttons, bow tie, hair band and hair scrunch shown here are just a few ideas.
(Left)

Bags & shoes

Bags and shoes may not be the first things you would think of embellishing, but they benefit from some individual creativity as much as any other accessory. Everyone has an outdated pair of shoes or a discarded handbag which can be recycled and rejuvenated for a new look, or you can buy cheap items in the sales or from second-hand stores ready for decorating.

You can cover shoes with special fabrics to coordinate with a particular outfit; treat the surface of shoes or a bag by dyeing, bleaching and printing; paint a fabric surface with fabric pens, glitter and glue, or expanding paints; or attach all manner of embellishments. Most fabric shoes and bags can be transformed with beads, sequins, buttons and embroidery, and detachable pompoms, buckles and bows can be selected to suit different occasions.

Clear plastic has been used here to construct a duffle bag, shoulder purse and clutch bag. They are appliquéd with sweet (candy) designs and held together with rivets, syphoning tubes and large eyelets. (*Below: Julie Nock*)

A gentleman's smoking cap and slippers made in wine-coloured velvet with old-gold appliquéd leaves and light-gold bonded appliquéd spirals. (*Above: Sarah King*)

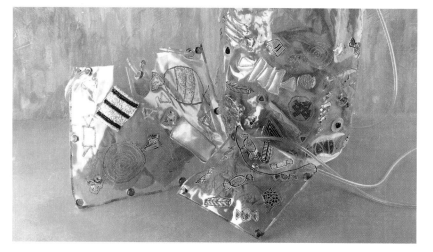

Decorating *Ballet pumps*

MATERIALS & EQUIPMENT

ballet pumps, dyed with shoe dyes
coloured pipe cleaners
needle and thread
pompoms
glue
embroidered motifs
gold braid

1 Twist the coloured pipe cleaners into spirals and zigzags, or a variety of shapes, as you wish.

2 Position the pipe cleaners on the pumps and oversew in place with matching thread.

3 Stick coloured pompoms over the pumps with glue.

4 For another idea, stitch an embroidered motif to the front of each pump. Cut two lengths of gold braid, and carefully stitch this around the edge of each pump.

5 Cover the joins at the back of the pumps with smaller motifs in the same design.

*H*ere two soft velvet drawstring evening bags have been embellished with appliqué stars and machine embroidery. The slub silk ties have been decorated in the same way using floral motifs.
(Opposite: Jacqueline Farrell)

Embellishing clothes

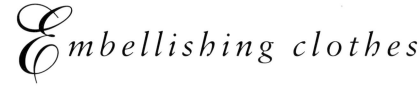

*B*utton covers are a clever idea for instantly updating or changing the style of a garment. The ones shown here are jewel-like and sophisticated, but the range includes anything from jelly beans to Coke bottle tops and theatrical happy and sad masks.
(Right: Johnny Loves Rosie)

It is the embellishing of an outfit, the adding of accessories, which transforms the utilitarian into something special and covetable. The plainest of garments can be customized into a walking work of art with a whole variety of applied decoration – beads, motifs, lace, sequins, studs and diamanté – and with a whole range of techniques, including appliqué, machine embroidery, hand-sewing and fabric painting. The decoration can be applied directly to the garment for a permanent new look or on to detachable panels for a temporary change of style. Here are just a few ideas to inspire you to get out your needles, threads and a host of decorations.

*T*hese exquisite pieces of embroidery, including appliquéd brooches, hair slide (barrette) and waist-coat trims, are made from velvet, felt and organza. Each piece is built up in layers and then couched with metallic thread and machine embroidery. The same design could also be used to create button covers, cuff links and shoe decorations with a suitable jewellery finding attached to the back.
(Right: Abigail Mill)

Heart *Trims*

1 Cut out velvet heart shapes and pin them on to the red felt. Machine stitch around the edges, then embroider the hearts with decorative swirls. Cut out the hearts.

2 Layer rectangular pieces of silk and metallic organza over a larger rectangle of green felt. Machine stitch in place around the edge and then stitch the outline of three squares on the rectangle. Lay smaller squares of metallic organza within each panel and machine-embroider around the edges with metallic thread.

MATERIALS & EQUIPMENT

small pieces of deep red velvet
scissors
red and green felt
sewing machine
coloured threads
metallic organza
silk
metallic thread
brooch backs

3 Machine stitch the red velvet hearts on top of the silk and organza squares.

4 Trim away any excess fluff or thread ends. Cut out the individual squares and stick a brooch back on the reverse of each.

*T*his unusual appliquéd tie looks stunning with a contrasting red shirt. Decorated in machine embroidery with a leaf motif and trailing stems, this tie will look equally good on a man or woman. (*Above: Jacqueline Farrell*)

A large-crowned hat makes a definite statement. It is decorated with woven button trims, made from fabric remnants and ribbons in plaids, checks and stripes which coordinate with the colours of the hat.
(*Left: Karen Triffitt*)

*T*his delightful smoking cap is made of silk, hand-painted with special silk paints in soft, glowing colours (see pages 38–41). The silk is decorated first, then the component pieces are cut out (a simple circle for the crown and a rectangle for the band) and assembled.
(*Below: Sarbjit Natt*)

A beautiful waistcoat and hat made from velvet and richly embellished with bonded appliqué, machine-embroidered into position. The colour of the old-gold appliquéd motif is picked up in the embossed paper earrings.
(*Above: waistcoat and hat, Sarah King; earrings, Gill Clement*)

Woven Button trim

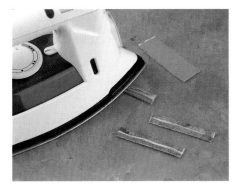

1 Cut a strip of fabric or ribbon to 2.5 x 14 cm (1 x 5½ in) and strengthen with fusible interfacing. Repeat with a piece of contrast fabric or ribbon. Cut each strip in half length-ways to make two narrower strips. Turn in the long edges so they almost meet in the centre and press well.

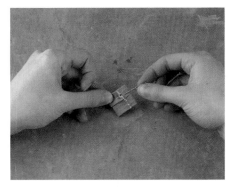

2 Cut out a piece of poster board 2.5 cm (1 in) square. Wrap two pieces of fabric around the square and secure by hand-stitching.

M ade from fabric remnants, these button trims are a great way to coordinate outfits. Attach clip-on brooch backs to make either shoe trims or earrings, or use small trims on shirt cuffs instead of buttons. Larger trims can replace coat or jacket buttons. If you want to use the trims on shoes, paint the poster board inserts with PVA (white) glue to waterproof them.
(Above: Karen Triffitt)

MATERIALS & EQUIPMENT

fabric or ribbon
scissors
fusible interfacing
iron
poster board
needle and thread

3 Weave the contrasting strips through at the front and secure in the same way at the back.

4 Oversew the outside edges securely to hide the raw edges of the contrasting strips.

Children's jewellery

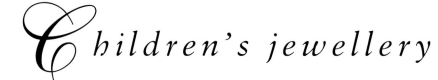

These appealing animal-shaped brooches are cut from plywood and brightly decorated with painted patterns. Brooch backs are simply glued to the backs to complete them. (*Right: Gill Hancock*)

Jewellery made for children needs to be easy to wear so that it does not catch on things while they are playing. It should be light, non-breakable and, in the case of necklaces, threaded securely. Polymer clay is a great modelling material for children to use for making their own brooches, beads and badges.

Make an edible necklace or bracelet by threading small sweets (candies) on to shirring elastic. The obvious choice for sweets for threading are those with a ready-made hole in the centre. However, soft jelly and candy sweets can be pierced with a needle and thread. If you want to make a necklace to keep rather than eat, cover the sweets with a coat of acrylic or clear nail varnish – and make sure your child knows that they are no longer edible.

For other ideas, look for decorative items in stationery departments: brightly coloured plastic-coated or metal paperclips can be simply linked together; or miniature clothes pins or plastic pegs can be clipped on to a cord to make a fun necklace.

These beads look similar to the decorated felt balls, but are made from quite different materials. The necklaces at top and bottom are made from wood decorated with paper cut-outs, and the hanging decoration on the top necklace is made from papier mâché. The necklace to the right of the picture is made from polymer clay. (*Left: Deirdre Hawken*)

Cotton-ball $\mathcal{N}$ecklace

$\mathcal{A}$lthough quite large, these cotton waste balls weigh next to nothing and are inexpensive; decorated in bright colours with a combination of emulsion (latex) paint and felt, they are ideal for children to make and wear.

(Left: Petra Boase)

MATERIALS & EQUIPMENT

several lengths of wire
block of florists' foam
cotton and paper waste balls
emulsion (latex) or acrylic paints
paintbrushes
felt in various colours
scissors and pinking shears
glue
coloured pipe cleaners
silver cord

1 Stick a wire into the florists' foam and push a ball on top. Paint and leave to dry.

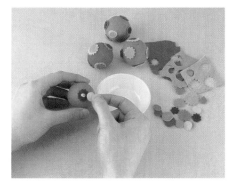

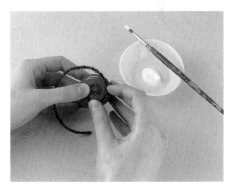

2 To decorate, cut out circles of felt, some with scissors and some with pinking shears, and some a little larger than the others. Stick these all over the painted balls, overlaying larger circles with smaller ones.

3 Paint squiggles, dots and patterns on to some of the balls in contrasting colours.

4 You could also glue coloured pipe cleaners so that they spiral around the balls. Thread the balls on to the silver cord, alternating the felt- and paint-decorated balls. Simply tie the ends in a bow to wear.

Natural & organic Jewellery

The 'back to nature' theme which is so strongly represented in many fashion articles today, whether in the materials used to create them or in the organic nature of the style, is clearly a reflection of the current growing concern and respect for all things natural.

For your own natural jewellery, look for shells, bits of driftwood, feathers, bamboo, pieces of bone, seeds or even small pebbles with holes. With the exception of the pebbles, all of these may be turned into beads by drilling a small hole using the tiniest drill bit you can find. Thread your 'found' beads on to raffia, leather cords or shoelaces to create an ethnic look.

Raffia earrings

These lightweight fun earrings are quickly crocheted in brightly dyed raffia. For a more elegant look, use natural undyed raffia.
(*Above: Rachel Howard-Marshall*)

Wood is the ultimate natural material. The top two necklaces are made from woods chosen for their distinctive colours and graining; the clean shapes show the woods to their best advantage. The oval beads in the necklace below are made from holly wood.
(*Left: Peter and Jacqueline Ridley, Heart of the Woods; holly-wood necklace, author's collection*)

MATERIALS & EQUIPMENT

3 mm (US 3) crochet needle
5.5 metres (6 yards) purple raffia
large-eyed sewing needle
2 silver kidney-wire clasps
3.5 metres (4 yards) green raffia
3.5 metres (4 yards) yellow raffia
3.5 metres (4 yards) red raffia

NOTE

When casting on each colour, always start 10 cm (4 in) from the beginning of the raffia, so you can neaten the ends later by stitching.

Abbreviations: ch - chain; sl st - slip stitch; sc - single chain.

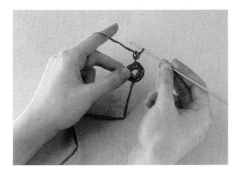

1 To make the main earring, using purple raffia, work as follows: 6 ch, sl st in first ch, to form a loop. 1 ch, 12 sc into loop, sl st in first sc – this forms the central, purple ring. 3 ch, sl st into first ch, to form a loop, as shown.

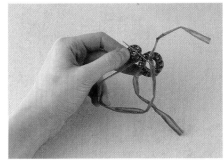

2 1 ch, 5 sc into loop (this forms the top small ring). Cast off leaving an end of 30 cm (12 in). Thread this end on to a sewing needle. Twist the end four times tightly around the join between the two rings to form a short stem. Bring the needle to the back of the work and stitch through the stem from bottom to top to secure the twists, as shown.

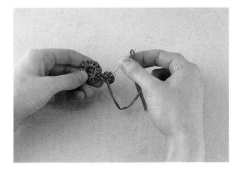

3 Place the silver kidney-wire clasp at centre back of the small ring. Oversew the wire into place, as shown. Cast off and trim the ends.

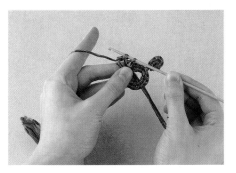

4 To make the petals, starting with the green raffia, work as follows: with the right side facing you, cast on into the 4th sc from the centre stem of the central purple ring. 5 ch, sl st into the same space from which you started, to form a loop. Working into the loop, crochet 10 sc, as shown. Cast off, leaving an end.

5 Thread a needle on to this end. Stitch into the space from which you started, through front to back. Cast off and trim ends, as shown. Using yellow raffia, repeat from step 4 on opposite side of purple ring, 4 sc from the centre stem. Using red raffia, repeat from step 4, casting on into the centre stitch between the yellow and green petals.

Recycled jewellery

Recycled jewellery can be made from literally anything: pan scourers, bits of telephone wire, plastic bags, electric cord and even balloons can be recycled to make interesting and exciting items. The most obvious recycled jewellery is papier mâché (see pages 30–33). White electric cable or fabric-covered electric cord can be threaded with coloured elastic bands; coloured or metallic pan scourers can be opened up to make bracelets; pieces of sponge can be cut into shapes and threaded on to string.

Another good source for original jewellery is Christmas decorations. The best time to buy these is just after the Christmas period when the shops sell off their excess stock at bargain prices.

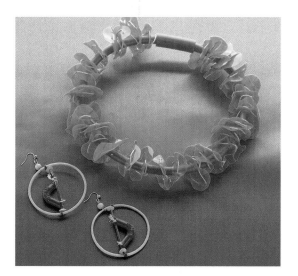

This necklace and earring set is made from recycled lurid pink plastic sheet, tubing and straws. Note how the corrugated part of a bendy straw is used as a decorative device in the earrings. (*Above: Deirdre and Anthony Hawken*)

Old grommets, telephone wires and corrugated plastic have been used to create an elegantly modern necklace and earring set. (*Left: Deirdre and Anthony Hawken*)

Using Christmas decorations

MATERIALS & EQUIPMENT

assorted Christmas decorations
scissors
impact adhesive
jewellery findings
embroidery thread and needle

1 The items chosen here comprise of a variety of hanging Christmas-tree decorations, including baubles, hearts, an apple, a train, and wired textile trims.

2 Cut off the threads used to suspend the decorations and glue clip-on earring backs to the red hearts and a ring base on to the apple.

3 Cut off the loops and add kidney-wire findings to Indian Christmas-tree decorations to make flamboyant evening earrings. Glue a brooch back to the train.

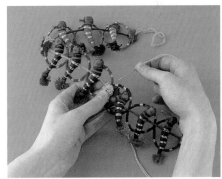

4 Gently bend wire tree decorations and sew them together using embroidery thread. Attach more embroidery thread to either end of the neck piece and wear it as a choker.

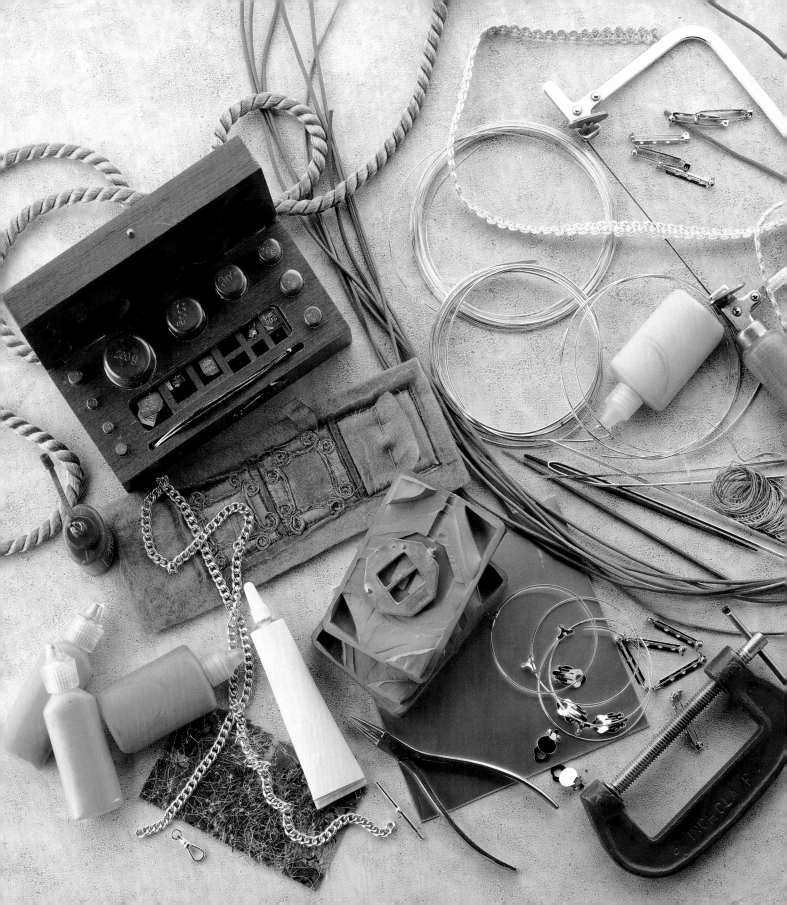

PRACTICALITIES

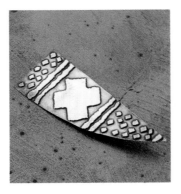

Do take some time to read through this section before embarking on a major piece of jewellery – especially one of the metalworking projects. Here you will find useful information on the traditional jeweller's tools, including piercing saws, tin snips, files and soldering irons, and how to use them correctly. The range of different metals and stones employed in jewellery-making is also detailed. Choosing beads to make jewellery is made simple with a listing of the various types available, and the main types of jewellery finding and their uses are listed and illustrated too. Standard jeweller's techniques, such as soldering, annealing, pickling and engraving are described and there are step sequences showing how to cut and finish metal, and how to make jump rings and a beautiful necklace clasp from silver wire. Closing with a look at storing and caring for your jewellery, this section provides a fascinating and useful reference source for the novice jewellery-maker.

Tools & equipment

As you will see from the projects in this book, you can make all kinds of jewellery with very little specialist equipment. The specialist tools and equipment described below are those of the traditional jeweller.

The work space

You do not need an elaborate work area to make jewellery, but do ensure that the work table and chair you choose are comfortable. If you are going to do any sawing you will need a sturdy table or work bench to which to attach a bench peg. A bench peg is a wedge-shaped piece of wood with a V shape cut out of it. This is usually clamped on to a bench or table with a G-clamp, and is used for sawing metal.

Piercing (jeweller's) saw

This is the single most important tool a jeweller needs. It is used for cutting metal and has a frame similar to a fret saw (scroll saw). There are two types of piercing saw, one with a rigid frame and the other with an adjustable frame. Saw blades used by jewellers are graded and numbered 2, 1, 0, 2/0, 3/0 and so on, with number 2 being coarse and the other numbers getting progressively finer. The grade of blade is usually determined by the thickness of the metal you are cutting, but there is no hard and fast rule. I suggest that you use a number 2 blade if you have not used a piercing saw before, as this cuts a good straight line and does not break too easily.

The blade is always placed in the frame with the teeth pointing downwards, in the direction of the stroke. Clamp one end of the blade in position, and adjust the frame so the handle of the frame is against the body, with the other end of the frame resting on the bench peg or bench. Apply sufficient pressure to enable the blade to enter the clamp within 1/16 of the end. Tighten the thumbscrew and release the pressure, leaving the blade under tension.

When cutting sheet metal, move the blade up and down with a slightly heavier pressure on the downward stroke. When cutting a curve, move the metal around while keeping the saw moving vertically in a constant plane. To saw the centre out of a piece of metal, you must first drill a small hole in it, and then thread the blade through the hole and continue sawing as normal. If the blade jams, it is because it is being held at the wrong angle. You can rub a blade with beeswax or paraffin wax to act as a lubricant.

Files

Although jewellers may use all types of files, those most associated with jewellery are known as jeweller's files

or needle files. As their name suggests, these are very small, fine files which are designed to get into the smallest crevice and the most difficult shape. They come in a variety of shapes including triangular, round, half-round, square and knife-edged. They are used for smoothing rough areas and to define shapes.

Tin snips

Tin snips are scissors for metal. They are most commonly used to cut a small piece of sheet metal from a large one. The metal is then shaped with a file or a piercing saw. Tin snips are also used for cutting wire.

Pliers

Pliers are used for metal- and bead-work and are an essential jewellery tool. As with most jewellery equipment, jeweller's pliers look like miniature versions of the handyman's pliers. There are three basic types of jeweller's pliers: round-nosed, flat-nosed and D-shaped or snipe pliers.

Round-nosed pliers have conical jaws and taper to a point. They are essential for forming loops as they give a rounded finish. Flat-nosed pliers are used to squeeze crimps, close triangles and bend wire. They can be used to hold a piece of work steady while using the other hand. Snipe pliers have serrated jaws and are used for opening and closing loops, gripping wire and squeezing crimps.

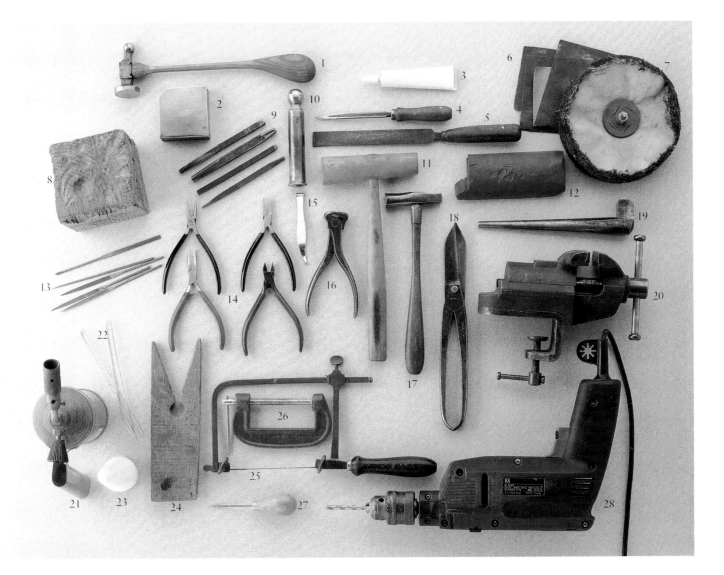

Jeweller's tools

1 repoussé hammer
2 metal block, for repoussé work
3 adhesive
4 scriber
5 file
6 wet-and-dry paper
7 polishing attachment for drill
8 wooden block, for repoussé work
9 metal punches, for repoussé work

10 ball-headed punch, for repoussé work
11 mallet
12 jeweller's rouge
13 files
14 jeweller's pliers
15 tweezers
16 snips
17 ball-pein hammer
18 tin snips
19 ring triblet, for making rings

20 bench vice
21 blowtorch
22 silver solder
23 flux, for soldering
24 bench peg
25 adjustable piercing (jeweller's) saw
26 C-clamp
27 bradawl (awl)
28 electric drill

Drills

A drill is used for making holes. This can be for decorative purposes, or to make an access hole for a saw blade so that a piece of metal can be cut from the centre outwards. The size of the drill bit determines the size of the hole. The traditional jeweller's drill is a bow drill, although a hand or electric drill may be used. The advantage of a bow drill is that it can be manipulated with one hand, leaving the other free to hold the metal.

Hammer

Choose a ball-pein hammer, which has a domed head at one end and is flat at the other. It can be used for beating and marking metals.

Sandpaper

Fine-grade sandpaper is used to smooth metal after it has been filed and before it is polished. The finest sandpaper, known as flour grade, should be used on the final sanding.

Polishing compounds

Professional jewellery-makers use a compound called 'tripoli' for their first polish followed by another called 'jeweller's rouge'. They can be bought from jewellery suppliers in large blocks, but they are inexpensive and will last forever. The compound is normally applied with a mechanical buffer. Some electric drills can be fitted with a small buffing wheel to speed up the polishing process at home. For small or awkward areas, the polish may be applied with an old toothbrush.

Blowtorch

This is useful for annealing – tempering or toughening – metal. A copper 'bit' attachment can be bought to convert the blowtorch into a soldering iron. The inner part of the flame (the hottest part) is blue, and the length of the flame indicates the amount of available heat.

Soldering iron

Electrically heated soldering irons are available in various sizes. A 15-watt iron is for very small, intricate work and a 100-watt is suitable for light sheet-metal work. Soldering irons are light to hold and easy to use.

Solder

Solder is the metal which is heated to form a molten filler used to join pieces of metal together. It is an alloy made from tin and lead and may contain other metals, such as copper. Solder is identified by its composition, with the tin content always being listed first, so 60–40 means that it contains 60 per cent tin and 40 per cent lead. Soft solders melt at a temperature below 450°C (842°F) and hard solders above 450°C. The solder must have a lower melting temperature than the pieces of metal being joined together.

Flux

Flux is a chemical compound which prepares the metal surfaces for joining, dissolving any oxides which might be present on the metal when it is heated. It also helps the solder to flow smoothly. There are two types of flux. The mild or non-corrosive type is used where it is difficult to clean a join. This must only be used in conjunction with a copper soldering bit, as it is inflammable and will burn if exposed to a higher temperature. Acid flux is corrosive and the corrosive residue must be cleaned off after soldering – this is easily done with soapy water.

TOOLS & EQUIPMENT FOR SOFT CRAFTS

Most of the tools needed to produce the craft-based projects in this book are, with a few exceptions, very standard. For example, scissors and a craft knife for cutting materials, a pair of compasses for drawing circles and curves, paintbrushes in various sizes for applying paint and varnish, and a range of needles (including an embroidery needle) and an iron, are all things you will probably have at home already.

The slightly more specialized equipment that you may need includes an embroidery hoop for hand-hooking and, together with a modern sewing machine, for machine embroidery. A special rag-rug hook is also needed for hand-hooking. For silk painting, an adjustable wooden frame, special silk pins or fine map pins, and a pipette or applicator for gutta are the special requirements. To emboss paper, a knitting needle is a perfectly adequate tool. A lightweight pendant drill is useful for drilling small holes, but a woodworking drill fitted with a very fine bit does the job just as well.

Materials

The materials used in jewellery-making are as wide and diverse as the jewellery made from them.

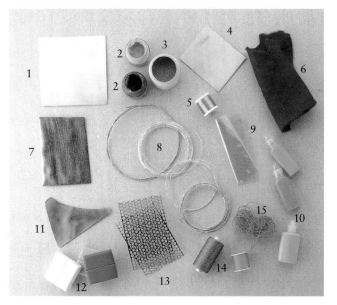

Jewellery materials
1 sheet silver
2 acrylic paint
3 gold powder
4 copper
5 metallic thread
6 felt
7 pewter
8 silver wire
9 soluble plastic
10 expanding fabric colours
11 brass
12 polymer clay
13 sequin waste
14 sewing threads
15 nylon thread

TRADITIONAL MATERIALS

Precious and base metals, precious stones and semi-precious stones, form the core of the traditional jeweller's repertoire. You may not be able to work in gold or mount diamonds and emeralds in your jewellery, but silver, copper and pewter and semi-precious gemstones are much more accessible materials for the novice to try.

Gold

Gold is a metal taken from the earth and it is known to have been used as early as 3600 BC. It is permanent, untarnishable, and so malleable that it can be drawn to a wire 150 metres (500 feet) long and gold leaf can be hammered to a thickness of $\frac{1}{282,000}$ of an inch! Gold is sold on proportion or carat value of purity. One hundred per cent pure is 24 carats. Gold fuses when bright red in colour and at a temperature of 1063°C (1945°F).

The legal standards for gold are 22 (fairly uncommon now), 18, 14 and nine carat. All of these are termed standard gold. The Victorians had a three carat which was bright orange in colour and was probably mixed with a great deal of copper. Alloyed gold can produce some interesting colour variations: white gold is produced with nickel or palladium; green with silver; blue with iron; purple with aluminium; lilac with zinc; and red with copper.

Silver

Silver is a beautiful white metal which is easy to polish, very malleable and ductile (easy to hammer or to draw into wires), and remarkably easy to work with. It has a very low melting point (961°C/1276°F) It has many of the qualities of gold, although to a lesser degree, at a price that is easily affordable. An alloy of 925 parts fine silver and 75 parts copper is called 925–1000 fine or sterling silver. The word sterling is the quality mark for the best silverware.

Copper

Copper is one of the most important metals for alloying with precious metals. It is easily worked, being very malleable and ductile and with a melting point of 1083°C (1981°F). Since 8000 BC, copper has been used in its pure state and as an alloy for other metals.

Brass

Brass can be used in jewellery-making but needs to be soldered with care due to its low melting point.

Nickel

Nickel is a brilliant soft, white metal and is malleable and ductile. It melts at 1452°C (2646°F) when joined with silver solder. It can be used on its own but is most frequently used as an alloy in producing white metals.

Pewter

Pewter is soft, grey and very malleable. It is made principally from tin with a little copper and antimony, while lower grades have varying amounts of lead. The best pewter is known as leadless, has a low melting point and is joined by fusing with a strip of metal which is not too hot. It can be cast, beaten or spun. Pewter can be bought in thin sheets.

Diamonds

Diamonds were originally found in India but are now mined in South Africa, Russia and Brazil as well as other places. The diamond possesses more desirable qualities than other stones and is found in a variety of colours, including white, black, yellow, brown, blue, grey and many other shades.

Emeralds

These are probably the rarest of all precious stones and are considered more valuable than diamonds. Emeralds are found in the rocks in which they are formed and, unlike diamonds, never occur in gem gravels. The most highly valued emeralds are those which are of an intense fresh green. Emeralds are much softer than other gems and easily scratched.

Rubies

Rubies are the oldest of all precious stones. The best specimens, found in Upper Burma, are a shade of red slightly inclined to purple. The genuine ruby is obtained from the mineral known as corundum and contains irregularly shaped air bubbles.

Sapphires

Often found in the same locality as rubies, these are next to diamonds in hardness and, like rubies, their value is determined by colour and quality. They vary from a light, bright blue to an almost black, opaque blue.

Pearls

Pearls have been considered splendid gems from earliest times. Pearl fishing has been carried on in Sri Lanka since 550 BC. Pearls assume every colour of the rainbow.

Semi-precious stones

As semi-precious stones are relatively inexpensive, they are an added bonus when making good jewellery. The infinite variety of colour, and the way the light plays upon and sometimes passes through the stones, makes them invaluable when making jewellery to fit a particular colour palette.

CRAFT MATERIALS

Many of the projects in this book use materials not usually associated with jewellery, and the range of possible materials you can use is only limited by your imagination.

Natural materials

A whole range of natural fabrics and materials can be used to make jewellery, including hessian (burlap) for hand-hooking, heavy unbleached cotton for machine embroidery, various silks for silk-painted items, raffia for crocheted jewellery and natural fleece for felting.

Recycled materials

Some of the projects make effective and imaginative use of recycled materials, such as sweet (candy) wrappers, foil packets and plastic bags for hand-hooked jewellery, or newspaper for papier mâché. Sequin waste, a very pretty metallic material with perforations which is left over when the sequins have been pressed out, can be encapsulated in plastic to make laminated jewellery or used with machine embroidery. The rule is, don't throw away your scraps or discard unusual materials as useless.

Wood, leather and clay

For wooden jewellery, hobbyist plywood, (a thin wood ply), is the best material to choose as it both lightweight and easy to cut with scissors. Thicker wood would have to be shaped by sawing. Leather scraps can be used to create interesting jewellery. The leather can be left in its natural state, dyed with special leather dyes or decorated with leather paints. Polymer clay is a wonderful material to work with. It is self-coloured and malleable when bought, and is hardened after moulding by firing in a domestic oven.

Resin-casting

Materials for resin-casting are a little more specialized and include rubber compound for making the original cast, and resin and hardener to make the cast items. Various coloured pigments and metallic fillers, in various finishes, can be added to the resin for a variety of effects.

Paper, poster board and pens

Paper and poster board have multiple uses in jewellery-making, from creating templates for use as a design guide to more decorative purposes.

A range of pens is always useful. Use a pencil to rough out designs, then trace them off over a lightbox using a pen; you can even colour in the design with coloured pencils to keep a visual record of your work in case you want to repeat the design later. A vanishing textile marker is invaluable for marking out silk-painted designs, as the outline fades naturally after a couple of weeks. Felt-tip pens can be used to decorate jewellery made from aeroply.

Paints

For painted decorations you can use standard emulsion (latex) paints, or acrylic paints, which are very fast-drying. For silk painting, always use special silk paints, which are free-flowing and intensely coloured. They can be mixed to produce additional shades, and they are washable once iron-fixed. Gutta is also used in silk-painting: it is used to demarkate areas of colour, and prevents the paints from spreading into each other.

This photograph shows just a few of the thousands of beads available. Many are shaped – look at the carved animals at top left and the glass fruits at bottom left. There are plastic, ceramic, wood and glass beads all treated in different ways, some inlaid with metal, others painted, cast into unusual shapes or dyed.

BEADS

Beads are an integral part of jewellery-making, and there is an incredible range of shapes, sizes and materials from which to choose. Here are just some of them.

Glass beads

Plain beads are usually round or tubular in shape with a smooth surface. **Faceted** beads are multi-faced and come in various shapes, for example round, oval and teardrop.
Bugles are long, slender beads, often used for sewing on to garments or hair combs.
Rocailles are tiny beads and have many uses. They are used in bead-weaving by Native Americans and were the basis of the beaded purses and dresses worn by 1920s flappers.
Shaped beads are often sold with glass or wire loops from which the bead can be hung. Shapes include roses, leaves, cherries, aubergines, bananas, oranges, strawberries, corn on the cob, grapes, carrots, shrimps, dolphins and miniature dolls, to name just a few.
Crystal beads are high-quality cut glass, clear in colour, producing wonderful rainbow effects when hit by light; they are usually round or a 'drop' shape.

Wooden beads

Unpainted softwood beads are round and are particularly easy for children to thread. They are ideal for decorating with paints.
Red wood is a close-grained Canadian wood. Although the wood has some red in it, the beads are a combination of warm colours ranging from cream and pale yellow to a warm rusty red.
Palm wood is cream with a brown grain and is made in washer-shaped, round or oval beads.
Coconut beads are naturally cream-coloured but may be dyed.

Ebony is a hard black wood which is sometimes carved, and sometimes inlaid with metal.

Shell beads

Mother-of-pearl is seen in its natural colour or dyed turquoise, pink, red, orange, yellow, brown or green. The most common mother-of-pearl bead shapes are round, but they can be found in almost every imaginable form from lovebirds to mushrooms.
Baroque or fresh-water pearls are nubbly in texture, creamy white in colour and a fraction of the price of cultured pearls.
Apple coral is red-brown in colour, often with black veins running through it.
Sea-urchin beads are made from the spines of the sea urchin and make beautiful dangly earrings.

Plastic beads

Plastic beads come in many forms, colours and finishes, including metallic ones. Some do not look as good as other beads, but many are well-finished and resemble the materials they are imitating quite closely. They are light, often inexpensive and do not break as easily as, for example, glass beads.

Metal beads

When one thinks of metal jewellery it is the precious metals such as gold, silver or platinum which spring to mind. However, base metals such as copper and brass are used a great deal for making beads. They are sometimes plated in silver or gold.

EARRING FINDINGS

For pierced ears you will need a stud or a hook (for example, a kidney wire), both of which are pieces of wire which go through the hole in the ear. Some studs and hooks come with a disc on which to stick beads, others have loops from which to hang them.

Earring findings for unpierced ears are either screw-on or clip-on; they too have either loops for hanging or discs for sticking.

Head pins and eye pins

Beads are usually threaded on to head pins or eye pins. These are pre-cut pieces of wire which come in various lengths. Head pins look like dressmaker's pins without a pointed end, and the beads rest on the head. Eye pins have a loop or eye at one end for suspending beads.

Bead cups

Bead cups sit on the ends of head pins, like miniature saucers, and are used to prevent beads with large holes from falling off.

Bails

If you wish to suspend a cone- or drop-shaped bead from an earring, use a bail. This is a piece of wire bent into the shape of a triangle.

Jump rings

Jump rings are split rings which come in various sizes and are used to connect one piece of jewellery to another. For example, you can hang two or three eye pins or head pins

from one jump ring and then hang the jump ring from the ear clip or wire.

Spacer bars

Spacer bars are pretty, decorative pieces of metal with loops at either end. They are used as an alternative to pins for hanging beads.

NECKLACE FINDINGS

Many of the findings used for making earrings are also used for necklace-making: jump rings and eye pins, for example, can be used in drop or pendant necklaces.

Spacing bars

If you are making a choker or wish to keep the strands separate, use spacing bars. These are bars with holes at regular intervals through which to pass the thread.

Split rings and bolt rings

These fasten necklaces. Split rings look like miniature key rings and are used at one end of a necklace with a bolt ring at the other.

Box-clasp fastenings

Box-clasp fastenings are used on multi-stranded necklaces.

Other fastenings

There are various types of screw clasps which may also be used to fasten necklaces, as well as hook-and-eye fastenings. You will soon discover the kind of fastening which is most suitable for your purpose.

WIRES

Copper and silver wires are the ones most commonly used in jewellery-making, and they come in many thicknesses. The thickness is commonly known as the SWG or Standard Wire Gauge, or dimensions are given in millimetres. Those most commonly used for earrings are 4 mm (about 1/6 in) and 6 mm (about 1/4 in). The 6 mm gauge is suitable for making jump rings or bails.

THREADS

When choosing threads for beaded jewellery, consider whether the threads are going to show, whether they are strong enough for the beads and whether they are the correct thickness for the holes in the beads.

Nylon gut is ideal for children to use, as it is easy to thread without a needle. Tiger Tail (a very strong nylon-coated steel thread) is ideal for heavy beads and can also be threaded without a needle. Fine brass wire or nylon thread is ideal for fine beads such as rocailles, and again it is not necessary to use a needle. Waxed terylene is a very strong, all-purpose thread which is easy to use without a needle and comes in various thicknesses. If you want to knot between beads for a decorative effect (see pages 62–65), use silk or thick cotton.

Leather cords are good for ethnic jewellery and beads with large holes. You could also use shirring elastic, or even lighting flex or cable!

Findings, wires and threads

1 leather cords
2 bails or pendant mounts
3 bead cups
4 nylon thread
5 wire
6 jump or split rings
7 diamanté
8 cuff-link findings
9 tug ends
10 spacing bars
11 box-clasp fasteners
12 string
13 earloop hangers
14 ear wires
15 screw fasteners
16 sleepers
17 plastic ear-wire scrolls
18 head pins
19 ear clips
20 brooch backs
21 button covers
22 tie-pin caps
23 tie pins
24 tags
25 eye pins
26 ear hangers
27 chains
28 hair-slide (barrette) fittings
29 display pad
30 necklet ends
31 bell caps
32 bolt rings
33 fish-hook wires
34 ear screws
35 metal ear-wire scrolls

Basic techniques

The following are all metalworking techniques, some of which you will be able to practise and perfect at home – indeed several of them have appeared in the metalwork-based projects earlier in the book. Others are more complex, and would require some instruction and access to specialist equipment.

Soldering

Soldering is a simple method of joining two pieces of metal together by means of a molten metal filler. There are three essentials for soldering: solder (metal filler), flux (a chemical compound) and heat. There are different types of solders and fluxes, and the heat is provided by either a soldering iron or a blowtorch (see page 110). The three elements must be combined in the correct way to suit the metal being soldered. There are three requirements for a perfect solder: the surfaces to be joined must be free from grease, dirt and oxides; the joins must be perfectly fitted – the closer the join, the neater the soldering; and heat must be applied slowly and with not too fierce a flame.

The copper 'bit' is the working end of the soldering iron and must be clean before you begin work. Remove all traces of dirt with a metal file. Heat the bit and dip it into the flux. Then apply the solder; let the solder melt and cover the working tip of the soldering iron. The iron is now ready to use. Always wear a face-mask and goggles when soldering: flux gives off fumes. It is also advisable to wear protective gloves as the metal can get very hot during soldering.

Lost-wax casting

There are various methods of shaping metals and casting is one of the oldest. It was first mastered in Mesopotamia more than 5,000 years ago.

The benefit of casting is that, once a mould has been made, many casts can be made from the same mould. This is a difficult process to carry out at home and needs some specialist equipment. However, you can make your shape and ask a specialist caster to carry out the work for you.

The most usual way of casting is 'cire perdue' or the lost-wax method. This involves making a positive shape, then covering this with rubber to make a mould. The mould is then cut in half and the positive removed. A number of moulds are made in this way. Wax replicas are then made in the rubber moulds. The wax replicas are put on a 'tree' with sprues and placed in an investment mould with a header to hold the metal.

A first coating of plaster is carefully applied with a brush to make sure that there are no air bubbles. The wax tree is then surrounded with hard plaster which is left to set. The plaster mould is then brought slowly to a red heat and the wax is expelled and replaced with molten metal. This is done under centrifugal pressure which pushes the metal into every crevice of the mould. When the shape comes out of the centrifuge it looks dull and is covered in burrs where each piece is joined together. The pieces have to be cut off the tree and then go to be finished and polished.

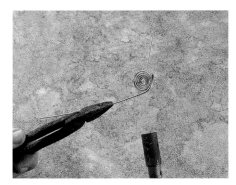

Annealing

Annealing restores the flexibility of metal after it has been worked. Various stresses are created during the bending, hammering, twisting and shaping processes, which result in the hardening of the metal and can eventually lead to the metal fracturing. Annealing involves heating the hardened metal to a certain temperature and then cooling it quickly or slowly according to the metal. This relieves the stresses and restores the workability.

Pickling

After metal has been heat-treated it needs to be chemically cleaned in an acid solution to remove firescale, surface stain and firestain (deeper stains below the surface). Pickling may be done in organic acids such as citric acid or mineral acids such as sulphuric, hydrochloric or nitric acid. Alum is one of the safest solutions to use in the home. Simply place the piece of jewellery in a heat-resistent container, cover it with alum and heat gently. Other alternatives are special safety pickles, or a homemade pickle – a solution of 1 tbsp salt in 250 ml (8 fl oz) vinegar.

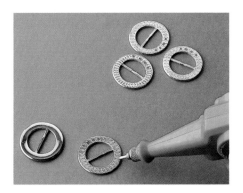

Engraving

This is done with a selection of tools: gravers, scribers, dividers, burnishers and scrapers. The design is drawn into the metal with a ball-point pen and then engraved. Use a graver to make the cut along the line you have marked. The graver should glide along the surface of the metal and throw up a thin curl of metal as it moves. Remove this periodically with a sharp upward flick. A scraper is used in the same way as a graver, but it makes broad flat cuts. After engraving, remove any pen marks with methylated spirits (methyl alcohol).

Repoussé

Repoussé literally means 'worked again'. This is a technique where a piece of jewellery is embossed or hammered from the front and back with special tools to give an indented or domed effect.

Chasing

This is a decorative design punched into the front of a piece of metal.

Enamelling

Enamel is a type of glass ground to a powder and fused with heat on a metal surface as a vitreous glaze. This is coloured by metal oxides, present in the enamels. Copper, silver, gold and steel are the metals most commonly used with enamel; silver generally produces the best result as it gives the greatest degree of reflection through the translucent or transparent enamels. There are five main techniques of enamelling: Limoges, cloisonné, champlevé, baisse-taille, and plique-à-jour. Of these the Limoges method is the easiest, as it simply involves shaking powdered enamel on to a base which is then baked in a small enamel kiln.

Cutting & Finishing metal

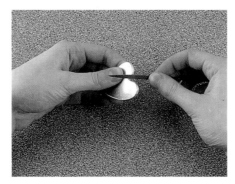

1 *A piercing (jeweller's) saw, used with serrated blades, is the traditional tool for cutting metal. The metal is held on a bench peg to allow the saw blade to be moved smoothly up and down.*

2 *Tiny files, known as needle files, are used to file the cut edges of the metal to make them smooth. They are particularly good for getting into small indentations, such as in this heart-shaped brooch.*

3 *When the metal has been filed as smoothly as possible, it is ready for polishing. This is done with jeweller's rouge and, in the trade, a special buffing machine. If you are working at home, a soft cloth will suffice.*

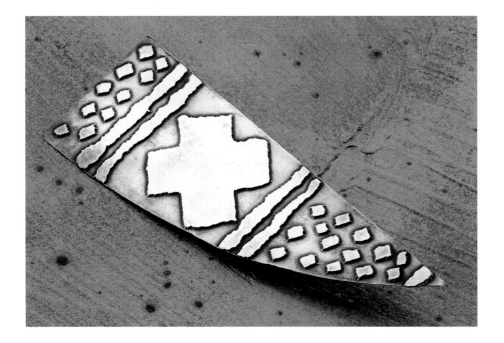

Simple-shaped pieces of metal jewellery, as here, may be cut with scissor-like tools known as snips. This is much easier than using a piercing saw. As long as you file the edges well, it will be impossible to tell the work was not sawn.
(*Left:*
Hammie Tappenden)

Making a *Clasp* and jump rings

Although it is easier to buy clasps, if you are stringing a necklace of very special beads it is well worthwhile making a beautiful clasp of the appropriate size. This design is by Alexandra Raphael.

MATERIALS & EQUIPMENT

10 cm (4 in) length of silver wire (the gauge will depend on the weight of the beads – use a thicker-gauge wire for heavier beads)

tweezers

small hand-held butane torch

matches

round-nosed and flat-nosed pliers

snips

silver polish and a soft cloth

1 Hold the wire in tweezers close to the bright blue edge of the inner flame. Heat the wire until it goes red and a ball forms at the end.

2 Bend the wire 1 cm (½ in) from the end using the round-nosed pliers – choose the part of the pliers to suit the size of loop you need.

3 Bend a small loop at the other end and cut off the spare wire using snips. Straighten the loop with flat-nosed pliers.

4 Make jump rings by bending wire around the pliers until you have what looks like a spring. Each complete turn will make a separate jump ring. Cut up the centre of the 'spring' to make lots of small unjoined circles. Push each circle so that it closes and is as close together as possible. Polish with a soft cloth and silver polish.

Caring for jewellery

Although some jewellery is obviously beyond the repair of the inspired amateur and is best left to the professional, there are some pieces which can be restored at home. For example, you could easily re-string a necklace, following the instructions on pages 63–65, or replace a broken jewellery finding. Often the only restoration needed is a thoroughly good clean. It is important that the mildest cleaning materials are used for this.

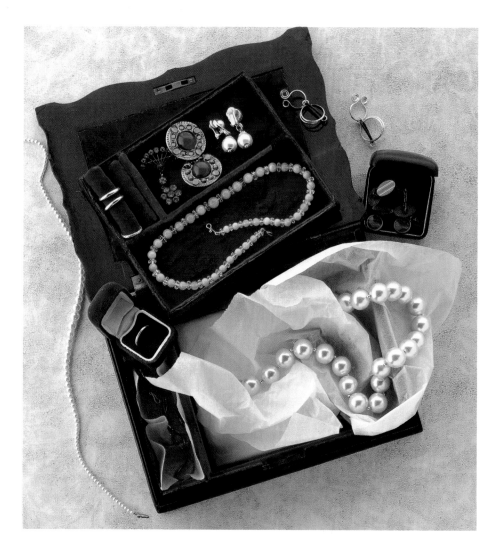

Gold and silver

Unlike other metals, gold does not tarnish. It can be washed in warm soapy water and rubbed with an old toothbrush or make-up brush to clean out nooks and crannies. Jeweller's rouge can be rubbed on to the metal to give it a shine. Silver becomes tarnished when exposed to the air, but it too can be polished using jeweller's rouge or silver polish.

Enamel

Enamel is usually mounted as a panel on to a metal (often silver) surround. Always check before cleaning that the enamel is not flaking away. If it is, leave it for an expert to clean. The best way to clean enamel is to wipe it gently with acetone using a soft cloth. Enamel can also be cleaned with a cotton ball dipped in mild soap and water, but the piece must be dried immediately after cleaning. Do not clean cracked or bent areas.

Base metal

Brass, pewter and tin can all be cleaned with metal polish, but take care as these polishes are abrasive.

*J*ewellery should be kept in separate compartments, ideally in a specially designed box with a lift-off lid in the centre and special compartments for small items.

(*Left*)

Shell, tortoiseshell and horn

Apart from washing, there is very little you can do to clean these natural materials. Shell and horn should be cleaned in a mild detergent-and-water solution using a cotton ball which has been wrung out. Dry shell and horn immediately after cleaning with a soft cotton cloth. Tortoiseshell should be cleaned with a mild soap-and-water solution.

To restore the lustre to tortoiseshell and horn, wipe them with a soft cloth dipped in almond oil. Use an artist's paintbrush to clean out the insides of individual shells before washing with soap and water.

Tortoiseshell, horn and shell may all be mended using epoxy resin glue.

Ivory and bone

Ivory reacts badly to exposure to both moisture and heat. It swells and shrinks, which can cause splits and cracks. For this reason, ivory should never be kept in direct sunlight or near a radiator or other heat source. Sunlight will also bleach ivory.

Both ivory and bone are best stored loosely wrapped in acid-free tissue paper to prevent mould from developing. To clean ivory, first brush the surface and then wipe with a cotton ball dipped in warm soapy water and squeezed out. Rinse with a cotton ball dipped in water and squeezed out, and dry carefully with a soft cloth. Rubbing with a cloth dipped in a little almond oil will both clean and restore ivory.

Ivory can be mended with epoxy resin or white glue.

Mother-of-pearl

This is a material which can be cut and carved and is often used as an inlay in other materials. It can be cleaned simply by rubbing with a finger, as the oil from the skin will remove the grime. It can be repaired with cyanoacrylate glue.

Pearls

Pearls are divided into three classes: natural, cultivated and wholly artificial. The best deep-sea pearls are liable to deteriorate unless they receive proper care. The brilliancy of colour and the lustre which makes a pearl so attractive soon disappears if it is allowed to come into frequent contact with rough surfaces, or to be dampened by perspiration which contains uric acid. Also, do not put on pearls before spraying yourself with perfume as this can affect them too. The natural lustre of pearls is sometimes lost by keeping them for long periods in a jewel case. A sun-bath generally improves them. Moisture damages pearls, so they should not be washed but dry cleaned in powdered magnesia in a jar and left overnight. The powder is then rubbed off gently with a soft cloth.

Emeralds and diamonds

The underside of most gems, including emeralds, is invariably open in order that the light can be reflected through the facets of the stones. It is therefore easy to keep emeralds or similar gems free from dust or soap by brushing the backs of the stones with rubbing alcohol or any other liquid which evaporates easily. Care should be taken not to scratch emeralds as they are softer than other stones.

The simplest way to keep a diamond clean is to brush it lightly with warm water to which a little soap or soda as been added. Dry from the back with a cotton bud (swab).

Amber

Never use alcohol or chemical solvents to clean amber as they affect it detrimentally, leaving it dull. For the same reason, amber should be kept away from perfumes and hair sprays. To clean amber, use a cotton bud (swab) dipped in warm soapy water and then wipe dry immediately. An old-fashioned recipe for cleaning amber is to rub it with some bread or almond oil. The best adhesive for repairs is cyanoacrylate glue.

Wood

Vigorous polishing with cream furniture polish or wax and a soft cloth is probably the best way of restoring the patina to neglected wood.

Storing jewellery

Jewellery should be stored in a container with separate compartments, be it a traditional jewellery box or a handyman's tool box. Chains should be rolled individually in acid-free tissue to stop them rubbing against one another. Rings are best kept in ring boxes. Never store two gold rings of different carats side by side; the less-valuable, lower-carat ring (a harder metal) will wear away the higher-carat and more valuable one.

The following templates are reproduced at 50% actual size. Scale up by hand, or enlarge on a photocopier.

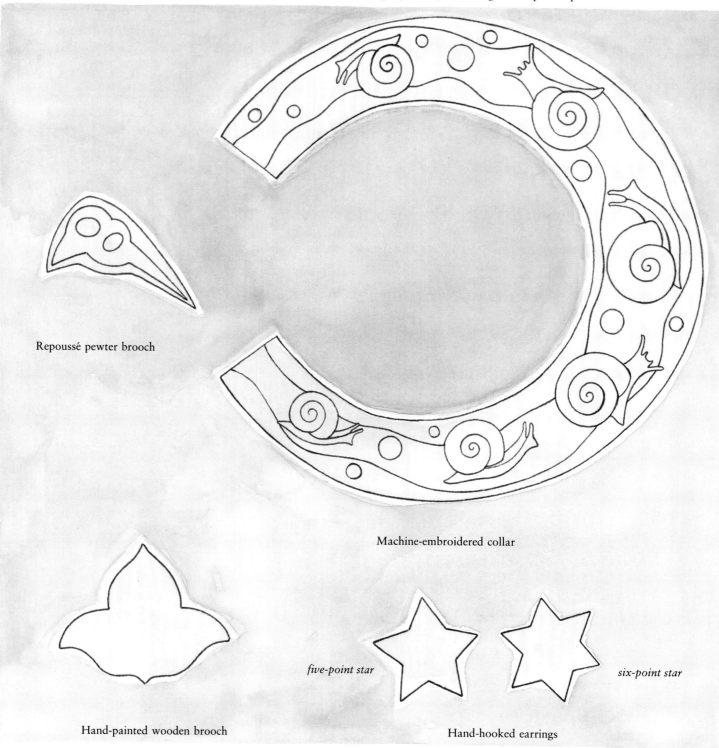

Repoussé pewter brooch

Machine-embroidered collar

Hand-painted wooden brooch

five-point star

six-point star

Hand-hooked earrings

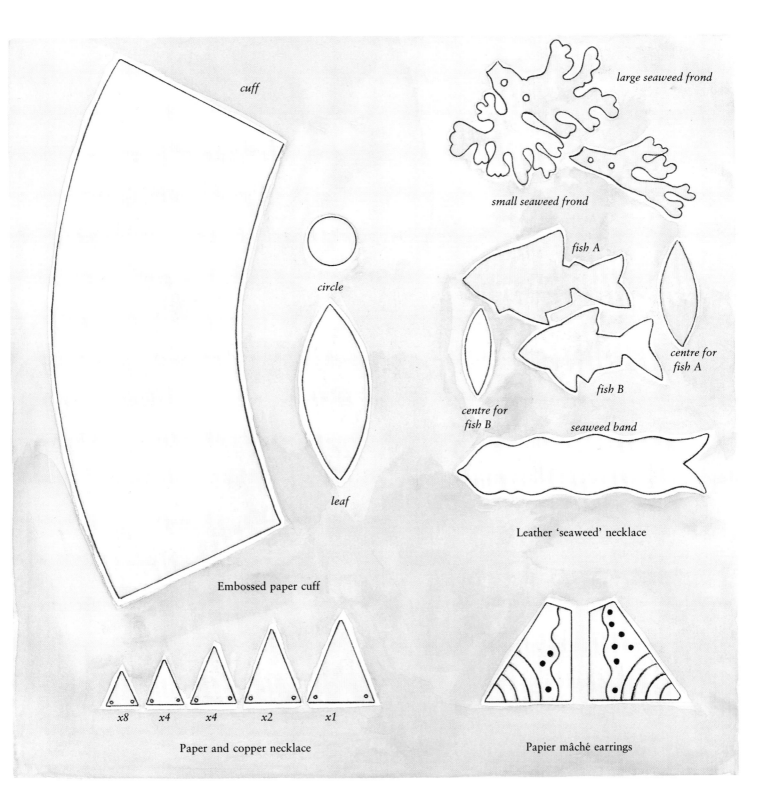

cuff

large seaweed frond

small seaweed frond

circle

fish A

centre for
fish A

leaf

centre for
fish B

fish B

seaweed band

Leather 'seaweed' necklace

Embossed paper cuff

x8   x4   x4   x2   x1

Paper and copper necklace

Papier mâché earrings

Useful addresses

Bead and jewelry supply stores have opened up around the country in recent years. You may find one in an urban area near you . The following is a short selection of mail order bead suppliers. You will find additional listings and advertisements in many craft magazines. One that is particularly helpful is *Ornament* (available at news-stands, by writing to P.O. Box 2349, San Marcos, CA 92079-2349, or by calling 1-800-888-8950).

For a more extensive list, you may want to purchase the following publication, a comprehensive listing of bead suppliers in the U.S., Canada, and England. Send $14.95 plus $2.00 for shipping and handling to: *The Bead Directory*, P.O. Box 10103 Oakland, CA 94610

Garden of Beaden'
P.O. Box 1535,
Redway, CA 95560
707-923-9120
(Large assortment of beads, supplies, and findings. Send $2.00 for a current catalog.)

International Beadtrader Inc
3435 South Broadway
Englewood, CA 80110
303-781-8335
(Beads, findings, supplies. Send $3.00 for a catalog.)

KUMA Beads
P.O. Box 2719
Glenville, NY 12325
518-384-0110
(Beads, findings, tools, books, and jewelry supplies. Send $2.00 for a catalog.)

Shipwreck Beads
2727 Westmoor Ct. SW
Olympia, WA 98502
206-754-2323
(Thousands of imported glass beads. Send $3.00 for a catalog.)

The Bead Shop
177 Hamilton Ave.
Palo Alto, CA 94301
415-328-7925
Beads, kits, findings, books. Send $3.00 for a catalog.)

The Nature Company
P.O. Box 188
Florence, KY 71022
1-800-227-1114
(Beads and supplies. Request a catalog or a store near you.)

TSI
101 Nickerson St.
P.O. Box 9266
Seattle, WA 98109
1-800-426-9984
(Jewelry-making supplies and tools.)

Bibliography

Bagley, Peter, *Making Modern Jewellery* (Cassell, London, 1992)

Coles, Janet and Budwig, Robert, *The Complete Book of Beads* (Dorling Kindersley, London, 1990)

Dublin, L S, *History of Beads* (Thames and Hudson, London, 1987)

Fairfield, Del, *Teach Yourself Jewellery Making* (Hodder & Stoughton, London, 1976)

Haig Milne, Wendy, *Making Your Own Jewellery* (New Holland, London, 1993)

Jackson, Carole, *Colour Me Beautiful* (Piatkus, London)

Rider, David, *Jewellery Making Manual of Techniques* (Crowood Press, Wilts, 1991)

Tomalin, Stefany, *Beads!* (David and Charles, Devon, 1988)

Wicks, Sylvia, *Jewellery Making Manual* (Macdonald Illustrated, London, 1985)

*H*ere are examples of using nature as it is found. Perspex (acrylic) and slate are cut into geometric shapes as backgrounds for sea-tumbled stones and pebbles. The stones are tied in position with nylon thread.
(*Right: Louise Slater*)

Contributors

PROJECTS

Deborah Alexander, The Polyclay Studio,
14 Barrington Road, Horsham
W Sussex RH13 5SN. Tel: 0403 241563

Helen Banzhaf, 31 Lampmead Road
Lee, London SE12 8QJ. Tel: 081-852 9672

Petra Boase, Rose Abbey Farmhouse,
Woodditton, Nr Newmarket,
Suffolk CB8 9SQ. Tel: 0638 730039

Victoria Brown, 88 Lyndhurst Grove,
London SE15 5AH. Tel: 071-708 5559

Anne-Marie Cadman, 232 Manchester
Road, Tyldesley, Gtr Manchester
M29 8NN. Tel: 0942 876182

Judy Clayton, 4 Burnside, Fleet, Hants
GU13 9RE. Tel: 0252 621609

Gill Clement, 8 Beaufort Avenue, Langland,
Swansea SA3 4NU. Tel: 0792 369759

Race Davies, The Basement Flat,
66 Princes Square, London W2 4NY.
Tel: 071-727 6185

Deirdre Hawken, 35 Glenluce Road,
London SE3 7SD. Tel: 081-858 7091

Rachel Howard-Marshall,
111 Dunstans Road, London SE22 0HD.
Tel: 081-693 0775

Rachel Maidens, 51 Devonshire Drive,
North Anston, Nr Sheffield, Yorkshire
S31 7AN. Tel: 0909 564408

Abigail Mill, Studio 10, Muspole
Workshops, 25–27 Muspole Street
Norwich, Norfolk NR3 1DJ.
Tel: 0603 760955

Sarbjit Natt, 20 Elms Avenue, Muswell Hill,
London N10 2JP. Tel: 081-883 4503

Heini Philipp, 188 Adelaide Avenue, London
SE4 1JL. Tel: 081-690 9808

Alexandra Raphael, 30 Kensington Square,
London W8 5HH. Tel: 071-937 3601

Lizzie Reakes, 68 Oaklands Road,
Hanwell, Ealing,London W7 2DU

Annie Sherburne, 4 Gabriels Wharf,
56 Upper Ground, London SE1 9PP

Karen Triffitt, Flat 2, 237 South
Lambeth Road, London SW8 1XR.
Tel: 071-735 0883

Rose Walter, 146 Westcombe Hill,
London SE3 7DT

INSPIRATIONAL

Stephen Anderson, 45 Ann St, Ipswich,
Suffolk IP1 3PD. Tel: 0473 213271

Holly Belsher. Tel: 0272 428905

Clare Dennis, Sundial Cottage, The Brook,
Old Alresford, Hants SO24 9DH

Jacqueline Farrell, c/o Harbingers,
431 Western Road, Glasgow G4 9JA.
Tel: 041-339 9999

Anne Finlay, 7 Bellevue Terrace, Edinburgh
EH7 4DT. Tel: 031-556 3415

Folds of London, 31 St James Drive,
Wandsworth, London SW17 7RN

Susie Freeman, 71 Sheffield Terrace,
London W8 7NB. Tel: 071-937 5254

Janice Gilmore, 28 Cyprus Park, Belfast
BT5 6EA. Tel: 0232 654867

Gill Hancock, Block 3, Upper Mills Estate,
Stonehouse, Glos GL10 2BJ

Heart of the Woods, 13 Vayre Close,
Chipping Sodbury, Bristol, Avon
BS17 6NT. Tel: 0454 311622

Johnny Loves Rosie, 131 Greenhill,
Prince Arthur Road, London NW3 5TY

Hilary Kay, Workshop 6, The Black Swan,
2 Bridge Street, Frome, Somerset
BA11 1BB

Sarah King, Waterside Studios,
Archers Wharf, 99 Rotherhithe Street,
London SE16 4NF

Debbie Long, 30 Woburn Court, Wellesley
Road, Croydon, Surrey CR0 2AE

Lushlobes, Unit 10, Giffin Business Centre,
Giffin Street, London SE8 4RJ.
Tel: 081-694 1664

Caroline Lytton, Bratton Court, Bratton,
Minehead, Somerset TA24 8SL

Gus Monro, available from Shanley
and Clark, Studio 13, Gabriel's Wharf,
56 Upper Ground, London SE1 9PP

Mandy Nash, Model House, Craft
and Design Centre, Bull Ring, Llantrisant
Mid Glam CF7 8EB.
Tel: 0443 237758

Julie Anne Nock, 3 Elcho Road,
Altrincham, Cheshire WA14 2TB

Rowena Park, 19 Goldsmid Road, Hove,
E Sussex BN3 1QA. Tel: 0273 746331

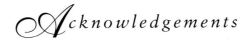cknowledgements

Sarah Parker-Eaton, 29 Morrell Close, Luton, Beds LU3 3XB

Amanda Peach, c/o The Craft Centre and Design Gallery, City Art Gallery, The Headrow, Leeds LS1 3AB. Tel: 0532 478241

Trisha Rafferty, Tichborne Studios, 18 Tichborne Street, Brighton, E Sussex BN1 1UR. Tel: 0273 327792

Mah Rana, 170 Brick Lane, London E1

Gaynor Ringland, The Black Swan, 2 Bridge Street, Frome, Somerset BA11 1BB. Tel: 0373 452952

Louise Slater. Tel: 081-748 6918

Kate Smith, 46 Crompton Street, Derby DE1 1NX. Tel: 0332 200830

Isabel Stanley, 5 Herne Hill Mansions, London SE24 9QN. Tel: 071-326 4764

Anthony Stern, Unit 205, Avro House, Havelock Terrace, London SW8. Tel: 071-622 9463

Hammie Tappenden, Seaclose Cottage, Locks Green, Porchfield, Isle of Wight PO30 4PF

Jessica Turrell, Zetland Studios, 7 Zetland Road, Bristol, Avon BS6 7AG

Karen Whiterod, Studio 10, Muspole Workshops, 25–27 Muspole Street, Norwich NR3 1DJ

I have enjoyed putting this book together, not least because of all the people involved who shared their secrets and time so willingly, and the artists and jewellers who entrusted their precious work to me for photography. My special thanks to them. The book has my name on the front but it is the work of a team. I would like to thank Judith Simons, my kind and understanding editor, James Duncan and Madeline Brehaut for the wonderful photographs and styling, and all at New Holland for having faith in the project.

The author and publishers would also like to thank the following for the loan of materials and equipment for photography (see Suppliers for company addresses):

Ali Wiser, Deirdre Hawken and Ann Scampton for the loan of their personal jewellery; Creative Beadcraft Ltd (jewellery findings); Inca (South American jewellery); Inscribe (polymer clay button backs and jewellery findings); Hobby Horse (beads and findings); Janet Coles Beads (beads, tools and jewellery findings).

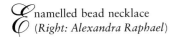namelled bead necklace
(Right: Alexandra Raphael)

Index